Dorking:
a Town Underground

Dorking:
a Town Underground

By Sam Dawson

Photographed and illustrated
by the author

THE
COCKEREL
PRESS

First published in 2019 by the Cockerel Press, Dorking

ISBN 978-1-909871-14-4

The Cockerel Press is part of the Dorking Museum and Heritage Centre,

The Old Foundry, 62 West Street, Dorking, Surrey RH4 1BS

Designed by Andrew Dorman

Printed and bound by Short Run Press Limited, Exeter

www.dorkingmuseum.org.uk

Contents

Introduction 7

Tales of mystery and imagination 9

The gardens of Eden 25

Digging for victory 41

Defence in depth 47

Trade secrets 71

High Street, low street 83

Tales from the crypts 95

Here runneth under 105

Beneath the law 115

Fields of stone 121

Taverns in the town 133

Hidden depths 157

Where to visit 160

Acknowledgements 161

References 162

Index 164

Introduction

Dorking is a small market town. It commands the Mole Gap, an invasion route through the North Downs dating back at least to the Romans. Part of the Surrey Hills, it embraces one river, the Mole, and a tributary, the Pipp Brook, whose multiple watermills may have helped give the motto to the town's literally riotous and later suppressed town-wide football match: 'Kick away both Whig and Tory; Wind and Water Dorking's glory'. For centuries, it was a staging route between London and the coast (Nelson trysted nearby with Lady Hamilton; Dickens visited the King's Head coaching inn, which became the Marquis of Granby in The Pickwick Papers). As well as being an agricultural centre, Dorking was a major producer of lime, sand, bricks and stone. Today, it's a pleasant town, known for its independent shops and at the centre of some stunning countryside. Less well known is the complete honeycomb below the surface.

Geology helps provide an explanation. The town rests largely on the Lower Greensand, specifically Folkestone Sand, a soft but stable sandstone that crumbles down into individual grains when excavated. It's easily dug: for profit, for storage, even for the bankrupting fun of it. Standing over the town are the North Downs, whose chalk has for at least half a millennium cast a similar spell over quarriers and miners. The legacy that this has left behind is a second town below our feet, a collection of tunnels, vaults, crypts, caves and cellars. At their best, each is a time machine, whose darkened and dripping interiors clutch closely onto decaying artefacts, masonry and carved signatures that would have been long since improved, jettisoned or lost if they had existed only in the world above. It is being hidden in the darkness that has preserved them. Many have lasted for centuries and, sometimes sealed and forgotten, may exist for centuries more. However, more have been lost in the last fifty years than in the preceding 300 and, in the last two decades, the destruction of underground Dorking has increased rather than decreased. We have inherited a unique historical heritage. It urgently needs our protection.

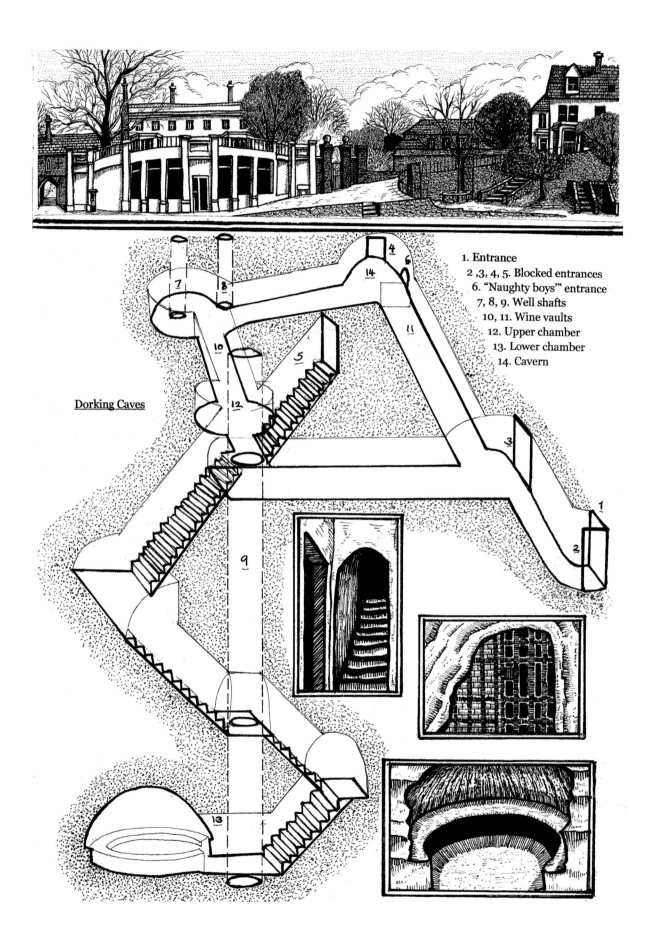

Dorking Caves

1. Entrance
2, 3, 4, 5. Blocked entrances
6. "Naughty boys'" entrance
7, 8, 9. Well shafts
10, 11. Wine vaults
12. Upper chamber
13. Lower chamber
14. Cavern

CHAPTER ONE

Tales of mystery and imagination

The word 'folly' comes from the French term for madness. It records an act of idiocy or insanity. When that lack of sense is cast in stone then the same word serves to describe the result: an expensive, unusable building of no practical purpose save that of satisfying the whims of its creator. Dorking is well supplied with these.

The jewel in the town's subterranean crown is the South Street Caves. Until it was widened in 1919 South Street was a narrow, picturesque thoroughfare, clustered with small houses and shops clinging on one side to Butter Hill. It had at various times contained a fine house and gardens, five taverns, a quarry, brewery, meadows, slaughterhouse, the town's jail, stocks, pound and poorhouse, the rural slum of Cockchaffer Lane, a distillery, the annual Pleasure Fair, dame schools, a tithe barn and fire station, plus the residence of Colour Sergeant Bourne of Rorke's Drift fame. There were also many small cottages, among which the caves' entrances were by then concealed.

The caves aren't huge, but they do have their own particular character and history. Little known, hidden behind a plain door, they tell a story of madness and industry. A tale of privilege, whimsy and eccentricity turned to serious use.

Down them once walked, or climbed, their creators: a periwigged and powdered gentleman, labourers hacking out the soft rock at his command, well-diggers, vintners probably worrying over the latest news from the war against Napoleon. All lit by the sparse light of flickering flames and all with sand down the back of their necks.

The tunnels cover four periods: the tree root-webbed 1921 entry passage, two Napoleonic era wine vaults, three wells and the 17th or 18th century original staircases and passage which one of the wells punctures. The latter are at the heart of the caves, yet who made them and when remains unproven. John Timbs, in his *A Picturesque Promenade Round Dorking* of 1822 wrote: 'Dorking being situate on a sandy rock, abounds with deep and capacious caves or cellars which are extremely cold, even in the height of summer. The most remarkable of these is one on the left side of Butter Hill, which runs for a considerable distance in an angular direction. On the side of the entrance, is a wide staircase curiously cut out of the rock and descending by 50 steps to a crystalline spring of water. About a century ago, an individual expended the whole of his property in digging this cave and, having just wasted several hundreds, he is said to have died in the poor house.'

The same story was told in the 1855 *A Hand-Book of Dorking* (whose author is believed to have been himself a resident of Butter Hill House): 'The large cellars or caves beneath the town, dug out of the sand rock, are highly curious. It is said that more than a hundred years ago, a man was foolish enough to expend all his property in making the largest of these excavations, at the bottom of which there is now a spring of pure water.'

Both books are vague about the date of these first diggings. Whether the story is true, and the core excavations were a rich man's self-dooming caprice, they were

Entrance to the South Street Caves and, behind it, the mansion home of their alleged creator.

destined to be put to use for a century and a half in a way that was already established throughout the town: alcohol storage. In the 1690s, diarist John Aubrey wrote that 'In this town, is a great Plenty of Cherries, particularly a wild cherry that Mr. John Evelyn tells me makes a most excellent wine, little inferior to the best French claret, and keeps longer; and no where are finer Caves for the Preservation of their liquor than in the Sand there'. (It has to be recognised that Aubrey's texts were edited long after his death, that he at times mixed up Reigate and Dorking and, as has been noted, he 'wrote largely from hearsay, and hearsay is not good evidence'.)

Speaking of sand, Aubrey was not above criticising the town's inhabitants, especially its womenfolk, for being insufficiently ruddy. 'The kine [kin] hereabout are of a sandy colour', he wrote. 'The women, especially those about the hill, have no roses in their cheeks.'

In his 1850 *A Topographical History of Surrey*, William Brayley strove for geographical, geological and historical accuracy. He too recorded the expansion taking place below the town from the 17th century onwards: 'Large cellars, colloquially named caves, dug out of the sand rock upon which the town is built, are attached to many of the houses. The most remarkable of these is on the left side of Butterhill; and at the bottom, a depth of probably from fifty to sixty feet, is a spring of pure water.'

The temperature in the tunnels is a fairly steady 14° C; just right for storing wine and beer. This probably led to their enlargement and maybe even their survival. Every house on the now destroyed section of South Street is said to have had its own cave cellar and all were lost, filled or sealed when the road was widened.

Right: Historic graffiti.

It's worth knowing that all of Dorking's 'caves' were manmade. None are natural. The term 'cave', which comes to us from Latin via French and Middle English to describe any underground storage space, used to be used to describe any cellar or vault.

We can be sure that the South Street Caves were used for wine, dairy and grocery storage but folk myths abound that they were carved out as a hidden church, for smuggling, or were linked to a secret underground river, or to Betchworth Castle nearly two miles away. These rumours tend to centre around the small chamber that is the caves' lowest point. The latter two theories are immediately provable as fantasy, the former two are highly improbable. Digging out the caves would have produced tonnes of sand that could not have been covertly carried down the busy street. Unlike in Reigate, deep mining can also be discounted. Greensand was used for glassmaking, water filtration and in high quality mortar and render. It had real economic value and could be sold by those excavating cellars to help defray the expense but in Dorking it was easily dug from the surface, and the town's geography is still strikingly marked by large, defunct quarries.

The later hiding of contraband can't be wholly discounted. The neighbouring hamlet of Holmwood was at the time mostly wild heathland and was reportedly involved in the trade, as it was in highway robbery. The tunnels *might* have been used for occasional illegal storage but the same is true of any cellar anywhere in England at that time. Similarly, it isn't impossible that the lower chamber, with its handy spring which could be used for baptisms, might just have found some use for covert religious purposes, albeit for a tiny congregation so suicidally reckless that they were prepared to risk trapping themselves below if discovered. It is doubly unlikely though, not just because the lower chamber would be such a perilous place for that purpose, but also because it might not even have existed in 1689 when the Act of Toleration rendered such secret religious services redundant. Dorking had a history of rebellion, freethinking and religious dissent. It hosted various nonconformist congregations, but generally in peaceful coexistence with the Church of England and Catholic parishioners. The only exception was an insurgent millennial sect, The Fifth Monarchy Men, who were repressed by the authorities as 'a menace to the public peace' in 1661, before the earliest dates in the caves.

Below: Guides' 'office', western wine vault.

Visiting the then closed caves in 1968, Chelsea Speleological Society (hereafter CSS) studied the physical evidence and determined that there were two structures in one: the wine merchants' tunnels and then the rest, whose 'shape and dimensions show all the signs of them being the mammoth folly of some person unknown'.

You enter the tunnels through a nondescript door that, when opened, partly covers a bricked-off entrance to a possible further void. Then a short pathway leads into the northernmost of a rough square of passages, and the caves' older, but not oldest, blocked entrance. It also allows entry, through a rusted gate, into the western tunnel, one of two additions built in or before 1815, according to the earliest carved date, for wine storage.

Like its twin, this is a narrow, arched corridor. Within them have been set 42 bricked wine bins, which could

Western tunnel, the wine vault, looking south.

have held up to 600 to 700 bottles each, in wooden frames. This brings the total for the whole complex to nearly 29,400 in the bins alone; more, along with barrels, could be held in racks in the passages. Like the rest of the caves, the tunnel's walls hold sooted recesses for candles, and acted as a magnet for historic graffiti. Here are the initials of previous owners and workers and tally marks easily scarred into the soft walls. The passage ends in a punctured brick wall that blocks, a little ineffectually, the way to the last corridor of the square, a small, rough cavern. This does not appear to be an intended part of the construction, but rather someone else's cave unwittingly broken into by the digging of the Napoleonic-era passage. It is that bit rougher, more rounded, cruder. The pick marks are longer and broader. Tellingly, it also has its own apparent sealed entrance, with the type of arched ceiling that usually signals a staircase buried below the sand. Plus a rather smaller and more recent one.

This is what is known as the 'naughty boys' entrance'. When the long defunct police station and town jail on South Street were demolished, a (now replaced) public toilet was planned, of the kind of plain, brick-built municipal design seen in thousands of towns. Literally bog standard. The story goes that on a Friday afternoon the builders suddenly found themselves digging into air. They had pierced the caves, then in their last years of fading commercial use. The workmen, wanting to get home, are said to have roughly concealed the hole and left. Over the weekend two sharp-eyed teenage boys did the opposite.

Reportedly they were found, hours later, in the nearby Meadowbank park, so drunk on the bottles of wine they'd taken that the police were called. They were taken home and the accidental way in bricked over, but not before the investigating officer squeezed through the narrow, crumbling aperture, to check for any further thefts.

By the light only of his petrol lighter he explored the entire complex, with its then perilously eroded steps, alone.

In a pleasing postscript, on a public tour several decades later, as the guide reached this point in the story, an elderly man is said to have put up his hand and said: 'That was me.'

From this point, it's usual to retrace your steps back to the northern corridor, possibly dug during the second, things-getting-a-bit-out-of-control stage of the folly. The corridor is arched and on one side has a flared shape that may reflect the caves' transition in Georgian times from caprice to storage use, the widening allowing barrels to be rolled into position. At its end a cataract of sand and antique broken glass marks either the deliberate construction of large storage bays or an abandoned attempt to make yet another entrance. If the latter, then the failure to punch all the way through to the surface offered a bonus: a brick-buttressed ledge enabled barrels to be positioned there for bottling purposes. It also allows us to look up at a revealed section of the ocean bed of 120 million years ago, complete with the wave marks of the Cretaceous era sea.

Cavern area with bricked naughty boys' entrance (centre).

The walls here also show traces of an ironstone often called carstone in Surrey It's a saleable, but rusty and less than beautiful stone, unless knapped, or galletted into decorative cubes and inserted into the mortar of walls. This may have reflected a belief that it created a barrier to witches, who would be unable to pass the metal. Certainly witchcraft was taken deadly seriously. Assizes records list the 1655 trials of two Dorking widows, Elizabeth Wood and Mary Walker, both indicted for having 'bewitched Thomas Bothell, who languished until 4 Apr. following, when he died at St. Saviour's, Southwarke'. Wood was also charged with having cursed Ephraim Bothell, aged 12, 'who languished until 23 Dec. when he died at D.(orking)'. They probably escaped punishment: nine out of 10 women arraigned for witchcraft in the county were found not guilty.

The northern corridor.

Above: Junction with stairs down (left), entrance to vintage ports gallery (middle), stairs up to the likely original entrance (right) – and above them all the shaft of the largest of the three wells, which appears at every level of the caves. Above right: Stairs to the caves' suspected first entrance.

From here the tunnel doglegs to the eastern corridor. A metal plate in the floor allows passage over the grandest of the three wells that pierce the tunnels. This will be met again twice below, and must have worked some magic on the caves' creator, given its ill-advised incorporation into the structure, which not only resulted in gates later having to be added to stop someone climbing down it to gain access to the cornucopia of liquors, but also to the flooding of the caves' lowest and most important chamber.

By the wellshaft, a set of steps rises to the inevitable brick wall. This may be the original entrance, sunk from the then substantial gardens of the Tudor-era mansion that commanded Butter Hill. It gives onto a crude, unfinished, circular, benched chamber, the larger twin of the one below at the cave's lowest point, 60 feet (18 metres) below the ground. It seems likely that this was the original core of the owner's ambitions: an inexpensive subterranean folly reached by taking a few steps down from his own grounds. A garden feature, a grotto or hermit's cave. The type of conceit you can find at hundreds of stately homes across Britain, sometimes with a statue of a water god, a tinkling rill or fountain, or a lining of seashells.

According to early chroniclers, the caves' construction ruined their creator. He supposedly spent the rest of his life in the Dorking poorhouse, which, cruelly, was situated almost opposite, a daily reminder of his pauperising madness. Did he descend to that first circular chamber to admire his handiwork, his private refuge, his unique hideaway, and instead hear a noise? Carts in the road, voices from outside? The inspiration for the artificial grottoes of the Enlightenment lay in the semi-mythical, spring-fed caverns associated with the divine oracles of Ancient Greece. Perhaps he pondered the proximity of the well and decided that embedding a live spring at its very source would add an even more impressive water feature to

Far right: The first sign of madness? The benched upper (probably folly) chamber.

his creation. Whatever the reason, he appears to have then changed his mind, turning from his original plan and going in the direction that very few of the grotto builders did: down. Deep down.

The stairs downwards are opposite the sealed entrance, just before the first attempted chamber, which was binned (literally) and left to storage and as an entrance to the later, second, eastern corridor. This was filled with more storage bays and is entered through a doorway marked 'Vintage ports'. It ends in a rough short space that doubles back to the cavern and the naughty boys' entrance – but not before passing two more wells. Which present further riddles.

It seems reasonable to assume that the three shafts predate the construction of the caves, especially the main one: there appears to have been a conscious effort to link to it after its construction. But the other two? Presumably they were originally from the cluster of cottages demolished after World War One, and appear to have been filled during the excavation of the Georgian 'vintage ports' corridor. Was one abortive, had they already fallen out of use, or been made redundant by the sinking of the third, large-bored well, whose wide diameter suggests that it was a communal resource? Or were they sunk as compensatory replacements by the landowner who wanted that main wellshaft to enhance and mystify his newborn classical labyrinth? We don't know.

Above: Vintage ports gallery.

What we do know is that the suggestion that the three wells are medieval is unsupported. It ignores the fact that the largest is actually dated 1672 and also that there was no known building in the field above until the creation of the first mansion on Butter Hill, well after the Middle Ages had ended. The 1649 manorial map shows only three buildings on this stretch of the road and one of those is the town pound.

One of the two smaller wells (far left); and its shaft going up (left).

What the wells do provide is a worm's eye view of how they were created. Their excavation is likely to have been the job of professionals, and a hard, wet, dark and cramped one at that. All three clearly show the alcoves (known as putlogs or putlocks) in the sides gouged out as hand- and footholds and to grip the cross-set timbers necessary for the diggers to return to the light at the end of each working day. These doubled as receptacles for the heavily-smoking rushlights or crude candles that illuminated their labour.

Two of the wells are filled in at this shallow first level. The other goes all the way down. To follow it, you descend a further flight of stairs, with a fairly high roof that suggests the steps were recut each time they became dangerously worn. These lower levels are the most characterful: narrow, darkened, and decorated with centuries of graffitti made by visitors and wine cellar workers. These carvings are surprisingly elegant; beautifully done, the letters almost all with serifs. Copperplate calligraphy rendered in stone by workers and owners, sightseers and deliverymen, and every one carved by the light of a burning wick.

Many of the names are traceable in parish, commercial and burial records, and even on the war memorial above. Kathy Atherton, in her book *Dorking in the Great War*, has solved one puzzle: the relationship between the final name engraved on the memorial, HH Young, and its namesake, confidently incised two storeys below, with the accompanying date of 1882. They were, it transpires, father and son. The former was Henry Harman Young, then a young spirit merchant, vintner and cave owner. The latter was his boy who, in 1915, aged 21, went missing in action at Ypres. The family approached the King of (neutral) Spain to inquire about his fate, and received the answer that he was a prisoner of war. In fact he had perished on the battlefield. Only in 1921 did the family learn how he died, when a German woman wrote to them. Her son, who had lived in England before the war, had found Henry dying from his wounds and given him water. He had asked his mother to find Henry's parents and let them know that their child had not died alone and uncared for. He himself was later killed.

Memorial to 2nd Lieutenant Henry Harman Young in St Martin's Church.

Halfway down the stairs is a further cutaway view of the main well. Beside it is a date: 1666. Then the stairs, with their heavily shadowed names and initials, continue down to the lowest level and the small, domed chamber that marks it, approached through the small antechamber of yet another excavation through to the well which for years drowned it.

This isn't just the caves' lowest point. It must also have been their raison d'etre. Their crowning glory, a humbly-sized Mithraic nod towards the underworld. The intimately small, igloo-shaped, benched room must have had some sense of mystery about it in its own time when, lit only by candles, it was approached down the picturesque but not entirely safe stairs. It is likely that here, for as long as his money held out, the gentleman creator treated his friends to an excursion below, at which refreshments would be served. Fragments of fine porcelain may reflect this (or they might equally be rubbish thrown down the well). It's difficult not to hope that something stronger than tea was served and that, before the owner was allegedly exiled to the workhouse opposite, he at least had a few decent parties down here.

I think it's possible that this mysterious final, rounded chamber might have been intended to resemble in miniature the Barons' Cave beneath the ruins of Reigate Castle and to tap into its legends of conspiracy and roistering. That neighbouring

town's subterranean structure was well known by then and would have been easy for an interested local gentleman to visit.

In England, the first half of the 18th century witnessed a succession of dry summers and droughts. From roughly 1750 onwards that changed, with a succession of wet seasons and heavy rainfalls, many of which ruined harvests and led to hunger in the countryside that continued into the 19th century. At some point after the caves' creation, Dorking's water table rose. In the darkness, perhaps unnoticed at first, the water must have risen to the lip of the spring, and then silently spilt over. The two lowest chambers flooded. There is still a very evident tidemark that climbs up the chamber's benches and rings the well. It is from here that dramatic Victorian tales of a sleek black river silently pulsing beneath the town emerge.

There are at least two claimed sightings of a boat sunk in this alleged smuggler's torrent. When you realise that any observer must have been standing five steps up, able only to see the well, awash, and the arch to the flooded chamber, you can understand the misunderstandings of hidden waterways coursing just beyond the candle's flame. An 1889 journalist asked if he could paddle just as far as the arch to see what lay beyond and was told he would sink to his neck in the freezing water. In reality, it would have barely reached his knees. Across the centuries you can feel his frustration: 'If we could launch out just a few yards we could see what is beyond that bend and we should probably find more caves.' Thwarted, he was told by his unreliable guide: 'You see (pointing to bits of mildewed board) the remnants of a punt that floated here'. And so the legend of the lost boat lived on. The best explanation is that it was an old gate or door. The water was still there as late as the 1920s when the *Dorking Advertiser* reported a visiting councillor falling into it, and a 1924 photo of the orderly and swept wine cellars (where did they hide the cascades of loose sand and the hundreds of broken bottles that are there today?) in the *Wine and Spirit Trade Record* appears to show clear water still lapping at the floor. It speaks of 'a wonderful crystalline spring', unconsciously echoing the wording of several Victorian accounts, including Charles Rose's reminiscences of the 1820s and 30s in his *Recollections of Old Dorking*: 'The crystal spring in the cave opposite was there then, and had been, in all probability, long before.'

Above left: A bankrupting act of folly? The caves' lowest and final chamber.
Above right: Ready to receive guests, the carved bench that circles the final chamber.

By the entrance to the lowest chamber is the bottom of the well which would later flood it, showing the tidemark left by the spring's iron content.

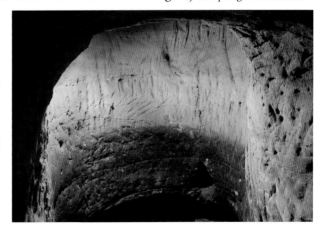

How long before is the problem. The story of the caves' origins as a local resident's expensive folly are likely to be true, but when he ordered their construction and who he was is less certain. The carved date of 1666 might be too good to be true: how many quarries and mines in the Home Counties aren't claimed to have supplied the materials to rebuild London after the Great Fire? Cliff Weight, who studied the caves with great objectivity, thought the first '6' might have been an eroded '8'. It also visibly lacks the elegance and ingrained sooty patina of the antique graffiti elsewhere in the caves. Despite its prominent position, it isn't mentioned until 1960. The *Wine and Spirit Trade Record* article, like others before and after it, lists the earliest carved date in the tunnels as 1753. There is a definite '1672' in the main well, but it is unreachable to anyone not working in the shaft. It seems likely that this date was incised during its digging, which could suggest a later date for the actual creation of the caves. Timbs, writing in 1822, said they were dug about 100 years before, which would fit with the similar declaration of the 1855 *Hand-Book of Dorking*.

During the 1710s or 1720s, The Great House on Butter Hill underwent major reconstruction, acquiring a whole new exterior, as well as a cavernous wine cellar. If this large and costly overhaul coincided with the overly ambitious excavation, possibly undertaken by professional tunnellers, it might have proved ruinous.

However, the facts point the other way. The work was commissioned by John Hall, Citizen and Guildsman of London, who bought the house in 1709 and went on to die, aged 88 in 1727, rich enough to be commemorated by a black marble memorial in the crypt of the parish church. This tomb was discovered and then reburied during an archaeological dig in 1974, showing how the town's interlocking history is revealed by a spider's web of underground connections. Time and again, an individual steps out of history in a subterranean context, then reappears linked to another underworld space, refuge or incident. It's no surprise to find that the eccentric Charles Howard of Deepdene House, another great subterraneanist, also lived briefly in this same mansion, adjoining the caves.

In the end, does the exact year of origin matter? The caves are fascinating whether they were begun in the 17th or 18th centuries. A precise date may be determined one day; it might only take the finding of a diary or a bill from a mining company. It is just possible that the story of a gentleman whose fortune was lost to the caves' creation may be based not on an owner of the house but on a tenant, but it's more likely that it has been grafted onto someone who in fact died monied and peacefully in a grander bed than any the Dorking poorhouse could offer. The meticulously charted list of householders published in Beryl Higgins and Vivien Ettlingers's essay *The Great House on Butter Hill* offers no obvious candidates for bankruptcy beyond John Ellis Stedman, 'a remarkably handsome man and as proud as Lucifer, [whose] overweening excessive pride eventually caused him to become insane'. He was committed to an asylum, but he comes on the scene in 1833, too late to fit Timbs' tale of hypogean hubris. All of which leaves former owner John Hall as a less spectacular but more logical candidate for creator of the caves.

Thankfully, more recent history is well recorded. In the old days Dorking Urban District Council kept a watchful eye on the town's subterranean real estate. In May 1880, the *Surrey Mirror* reported from the town's Sanitary Committee: 'Approval of a set of plans of six cottages (possibly Victoria Terrace) purposed to be erected in South-street was deferred to enable a committee to view the site, under which a large cave runs, and which, it has been suggested, may collapse should the cottages be erected on its crown'. They acted fast back then. Within a month a special sub-committee had been appointed, had inspected, and reported back. The group, made up of a collection of familiar local tradesmen's names, had made tracings of the cave 'so far as they could' and were able to confirm that the builder had taken sensible precautions.

The surveyor was back on the case five years later when he 'drew attention to the sewerage operations in close proximity to the caves in the town. He was of the opinion that the Board should become acquainted with the distance which would exist between the sewers and the crown of the caves.' The surveyor was just recovering from a bruising public confrontation with the landlord of the Wheatsheaf Inn, whom he had accused of excavating sand from his cellars under the High Street. He had not received much backing from his colleagues, as he had entered the Wheatsheaf caves without the owner's permission. As a result 'Mr. Maybank said the Board ought not to interfere, as he thought such caves were an infringement on parish property. Mr. Todman was of opinion that this was a proper question to raise, more especially from what he and the Chairman saw when some time since they innocently trespassed in a cave.' The fight had gone out of them. The paper reported: 'The matter dropped.'

In fact the fears proved realistic. In 1894, sewerage began leaking into the caves. The surveyor reported on the conclusion of the necessary repairs: 'The sewer was found to have sunk considerably, and this had been supported by girders placed on substantial brick-work piers, while the defective pipes had been replaced. Mr. Maybank asked by which contractor this sewer was originally laid? The Clerk thought it would be Mr. Bloomfield. Mr. Maybank said he never saw a more careless or more slovenly piece of work. The Chairman was afraid this was not the only piece of bad work by a good many. Mr. Maybank considered the Surveyor deserved credit for having called attention to the matter so quickly.' The surveyor had been vindicated. But there's no record that he ever went down the Wheatsheaf caves again.

In 2018, it was water that began leaking into the caves, at first as a drip and in the end like rainfall. All tours had to be cancelled at short notice while, in a near rerun of the 1894 incident, work went on to fix a valve in mains piping running above the tunnel ceiling to Victoria Terrace. There were fears that the flow could lead to an imminent roof collapse. Victoria Terrace, just a metre above the cave roof, was briefly closed. The valve was replaced. For safety reasons tours remained suspended from October until the following year.

We also know the names, addresses and specialities of the family companies that owned and then rented the tunnels in the Georgian and Victorian eras and beyond: Cheesman's (whose grand High Street shop is now one of three that makes up Boots Chemists), Young's (who sold them to Dorking Urban District Council) and HG Kingham's (who rented them from 1912, explaining the repetition of that date in the vintage ports gallery). All left their initials behind and the last was a prolific advertiser, leaving us the proof of what the caves once held. Interested in Very Fine Old Port Wines from 24 shillings (£1.20) a dozen? The 1887 Jubilee Vintage is just three and fourpence (17p) a bottle. Or German wine? Very popular with the gentry; Leopold Salomons, who gifted Box Hill to the National Trust, purchased prodigious quantities of it during his tenure of nearby Norbury Park House. Or perhaps champagne takes your fancy. The 1904? Yours at just 48 shillings (£2.40) for 12 bottles. You can even order by telephone. Ask the operator to connect you with Number 9 Dorking.

*Above: Rose Hill House.
A 19th century speculator
made two homes out of
the original mansion, then
added a third – the arch
house – to the side.
Above right: The old
mansion's Tudor staircase
found a new home in the
arch house.*

There are sure to have been customers among the generations of occupants of the by then subdivided Butter Hill mansion. In 1831, a century after the original Tudor building had been expanded and given its fashionable façade and bays, it was split in two. This was the work of Guildford surgeon and property speculator William Newland, and an assertion of the town's increasing affluence and popularity as a pure-aired country haven from the choking atmosphere and overcrowding of the capital. (As referenced in Jane Austen's 1815 novel *Emma*: 'Nobody is healthy in London… They had a very fine day for Box Hill.')

The division made two desirable residences out of one, and added a third to the side. In a pleasing echo of the eccentricities that created the caves, this new building was distinguished by a working folly that has become a modest town landmark: a gothic arch fit for a story book castle, which led to the substantial gardens behind. The apparently whimsical nature of the new building belies the workings of a hard-nosed entrepreneur. Its romantic historicism is likely to have been motivated by the availability of salvaged materials that no longer fitted the modernised residences. Into this annexe went the staircase, stone floor, decorative rose carvings and other fittings from the core 16th century mansion. As the current owner says, no window matches any other, no door has a twin.

Meanwhile, the two now semi-detached main buildings were let on 21 year leases, providing fine homes for those who could afford them and for their servants. The newly-named Rose Hill House institutionalised in stone and brick this *Upstairs, Downstairs* life. Its semi-basement cellar is warrenlike, now airy and well-lit, but previously a closely packed burrow of work and storage, a collection of fireplaces, kitchens, scullery, ovens, mesh-cupboarded larders, meat and cheese rooms. Deliveries came, out of sight of the carriageway entrance, down steps from the street and into below-ground foodstores, then to the kitchen, onto worktops and into ovens, and only then up a separate stairway and into the serving room, before finally being hand-delivered to the residents and guests in the bright, high-ceilinged dining and drawing rooms above.

Much of the servants' lives would have been spent down here, in rooms lit only by barred window wells, candles, and, later, oil and gas lamps. As owner Patti Lister said, referring to the 1970s TV series: 'You can imagine Mrs Bridges bullying Ruby down here'.

*Below: A nice (modern)
touch of humour by the arch.*

When this basement level was being restored, 34 skiploads of rubble were removed from a semi-enclosed, dense cluster of coal cellar, workrooms, storage rooms, outhouses, a brick-lined well, pens and outhouses – complete with cattle troughs, multiple meathooks and mangers – that housed ill-fated animals destined for the slaughterhouse opposite. The builders won the day when they said that it would be just too uneconomic to break open and return to use a further, sealed, earth-filled room with bread oven.

The same division of labour and light is evident next door, in what since 1831 has been known as Butter Hill House. Once again there is a strikingly large semi-basement, once given over to coal cellar and storage, servants' stairs and narrow passages, scullery and kitchen (with giant sinks and cooking range to match), and, like its neighbour, a further, still-sealed service room or larder.

Above left: Butter Hill House.
Above right: Kitchen range by Stone & Turner, Dorking.

The cellar at Butter Hill House was dug beneath the house's basement. The well it doomed is visible through the shadowy cavity by the stairs and through the hole in the first step's riser.

Above: The cellar, later a workshop and air raid shelter, was once lit by the gas pipe on the left.

Further down, there's a vault beneath the cellars, a classic Dorking cave hewn from the sandstone. This was a wine cellar, once locked and probably barred, punctuated with bays for bottles and brick platforms for barrels. Like the nearby South Street Caves, it is a treasury of graffiti dating back to the 1720s and hand-carved by those who once worked below. The owners' names are absent. Unlike the windowed rooms upstairs, where a name, dates and motto were incised in the glass, probably using a diamond ring, this was not a place in which they sought to be remembered.

A cavity to the side of the stairs and a small collapse below the lowest riser hints that there was something subterranean here even before 1720. An examination inside it reveals the outline of yet another well, rubble-filled, unwanted and enclosed by stairs in that decade, which would once have stood outside the original Tudor building.

Centuries later, with the driving through of a ventilation pipe to the surface, this cellar acted as the house's air raid shelter. Sadly, the possibility of a secret passage running from here to the nearby South Street Caves, their creator's personal promenade to his nearby labyrinth of allegedly ruinous madness, has to be ruled out.

In 1970 Dorking and Leith Hill Preservation Society took over the lease of the by then unused South Street Caves. They began escorted tours, which were made possible by Dorking council and, more recently, Mole Valley District Council, installing handrails, concrete steps and electric lighting. After some interruptions and

Right: The reminders of past eras live on underground.

an interregnum of several years caused by the closure of the local tourist information point, Dorking Museum now has the licence (and volunteer taskforce of cave guides) to once again offer access.

Far left: The caves are lit by electricity and by candlelight.
Left: Halloween tours were staged for the first time in 2017.

The insurance, health and safety and licensing provisions have clearly been formidable. The resumption of tours in 2015 is one small victory over the continuing loss of our subterranean historical heritage. It's also a modest triumph for the town itself, bringing in visitors and opening up a hidden part of its history to its inhabitants. People who came on outings as youngsters in the 1970s and 80s are now bringing their own children and grandchildren. It's a rare tour that doesn't have someone who mentions a cave they heard of or played in as a child or hung out in as a teenager. It all underlines just how extensive the hidden honeycomb beneath Dorking actually is.

And none of it is more extensive than what is below Deepdene.

CHAPTER TWO

The gardens of Eden

Deepdene was a phenomenon. So was its owner, the Honourable Charles Howard. It was a house that never stopped growing, set in sublime hillside gardens; he was a man of huge wealth, with an imagination to match.

Howard was a generous host who took pride in his creations. The result is that we have good descriptions of the house's first, of two, eras of subterranean glory.

In 1655, John Evelyn recorded that: 'I went to Darking, to see Mr. Cha. Howard's amphitheatre, garden, or solitarie recess, being 15 acres environ'd by a hill. He shows us divers rare plants, caves, and an elaboratory.' The laboratory was tunnelled into the hillside in which the new house so elegantly nestled. It appears to have been largely unplanned, with further, not always fully stable, digging being ordered on a whim to make room for a new alchemical furnace or foundry. This required the excavation of various airholes and flues whose arbitrary siting was reportedly still puzzling visitors centuries later. Walking the grounds today you still find unexplained depressions, hidden water tanks and fragments of decorative columns and urns.

Dorking resident Daniel Defoe was another visitor, writing that: 'The antient possessor, Mr. Howard, by what we call a perforation, caused a vault or cave to be made quite through the hill.'

If that sounds fanciful, then John Aubrey, who considered the estate 'an epitome of paradise, and the garden of Eden seems well imitated here', authenticated the claim. 'In the hill of the left hand, (being sandy ground),' he wrote, 'is a cave digged thirty-six paces long, four broad and five yards high; and at about two thirds of the hill, he hath dug another subterranean Walk or Passage to be pierc'd thro' the Hill; thro' which (as thro' a Tube) you have the Vista over all the South part of Surrey and Sussex to the Sea. The South Side of this Hill is converted into a Vineyard.'

The use of tenses is significant. Aubrey is writing about a begun but not yet finished project to create an optical tunnel, driven simultaneously from both sides of the hill, that would allow Howard to see the sea. (It wouldn't have.) Later accounts say that 'for want of an arch or support' the whole thing collapsed, burying the labourers' tools and only sparing their lives because they were at breakfast. The front entrance was converted into a shallow grotto.

That setback didn't stop Howard, or later owners. The digging of underground alchemical chambers – approvingly described by Aubrey as 'subterraneous grots' – continued. After Howard's death, aged 83, the estate passed to his brother, the equally rich Duke of Norfolk of Arundel Castle fame. By 1822 the property, with a fine new Palladian mansion replacing the original house, was owned by the mind-bogglingly rich Anglo-Dutch Hope family, the owners of the supposedly accursed Hope Diamond now in the Smithsonian Museum. According to Timbs, writing that year, the gardens are 'a kind of FAIRY REGION … with several ruined grottoes and hermitages … ornamental bridges, porticoes, lodges, green-houses, orangeries, pineries'. Within a few years you could walk twelve miles and not step outside Hope land. These were, indeed, the gardens of Eden.

Top left: The lethally dangerous hill-piercing tunnel was converted into a 'subterraneous grot'.
Top right: Brought back to the surface: Deepdene's sunken mausoleum is once more visible and visitable.
Right: Neither riches nor Polidori could bring him back to life: Deepdene's mausoleum, shrine to Thomas Hope's lost son.

The additions didn't stop there. In 1815, Thomas Hope built a temple, dedicated to his brother to thank him for spending the staggering sum of £30,000 on the neighbouring Chart Park estate and stately home for Thomas to knock down. That same year, he took his two year old son on one of his famed art collecting expeditions. In Pisa, the boy fell ill. Despite treatment by Lord Byron's physician, John Polidori, of *Frankenstein, The Vampyre* and Villa Deodati fame, he died and his ashes were buried back home, where a mausoleum was raised.

By the time Deepdene (now boosted by the purchase of two more major neighbouring estates and the demolition of their houses) finally left the Hope family's hands, it had become a confection of a house: a vast wedding cake of a structure with every wing, façade and chimney ornamented; a quiet riot of balustrades, columns, quoins, cornices, entablature and friezes.

In 1920, *The Times* astutely noted that: 'The future of such houses is for hotels and institutions. Deepdene is a place of great beauty.' The extraordinary grounds, formerly studded with antique statuary, had shrunk, but the building was as stunning as ever when, in 1923, it passed into use as a luxury hotel, with a telegraphic address that pleasingly echoed Aubrey's description of it: 'Eden, Dorking'.

Luxurious it was, offering 90 bedrooms, 26 bathrooms, courtly reception rooms, a ballroom, 50 acres of genuinely superb gardens, tennis, golf,

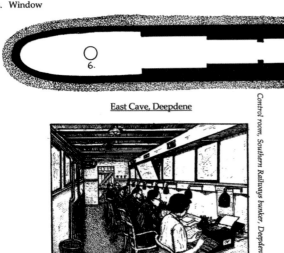

Deepdene Icehouse

The icehouse in the 1820s

1. Former entrance lobby with stairs down and temple-style façade (now collapsed)
2. Larder
3. Window

4. Corridor, formerly with large, twin hatch doors
5. Ice chamber
6. Escape shaft

East Cave, Deepdene

Control room, Southern Railways bunker, Deepdene

dancing and 'Recherché dinners at 7/6 to 12/6'. As its advert stated, it was 'Now open as a first-class hotel, and is the rendezvous of smart society'.

The hotel had everything necessary to succeed except good management. Its ownership was obscure, nominally in the hands of a Russian émigré, David Leonteivich Zhivotovsky, who had escaped the Bolsheviks and was at the centre of a dangerous mix of White Russians and ultra-nationalist exile groups subsidised by British Intelligence. However, behind the scenes was J Maundy Gregory, C of E clergyman's son turned atheist turned Catholic convert. Actor, theatrical producer, magazine publisher, nightclub owner, Knight Commander of the Most Noble Order of Pius IX, informant to the intelligence services, and Lloyd George's middleman in the honours peddling scandal. He had made, and continued to make, a fortune selling peerages on behalf of the Prime Minister and the Vatican.

Gregory was a man with no apparent redeeming features. Monocled, chauffeured, overdressed, a lover of luxury, possible pimp and probable blackmailer, he sold the personal information gleaned at his clubs, parties and hotels, especially that which compromised his fellow gay friends and contacts. It is likely that he was the man who suggested to the Secret Intelligence Service that they leak the diaries of Sir Roger Casement, reformer and knight of the realm turned Irish Republican Brotherhood arms facilitator. Their exposure deprived Casement, then on trial for his life, of the conservative Irish and American support he would otherwise have received, due to their vivid charting of his highly active gay sex life. Gregory was also linked to the disappearance of 'Labour's lost leader', the one-time MP Victor Grayson, and was investigated by Scotland Yard for the possible murder by poison of heiress Edith Rosse. When her coffin was exhumed it was discovered that Gregory had had her buried just 18 inches below the earth in a regularly-flooded graveyard just next to

Above: Deepdene's icehouse was built in the 1760s, but had a larder, entrance lobbies and temple-style facade added in the time of Thomas Hope. Icehouses are usually hidden and functional. Hope's was a showy, four-chambered, neo-classical conversation starter at least three times as large as the one at Wotton House. The icehouse's temple-styled frontage was demolished in the 1970s, leaving behind the unusual, multiple-roomed structure.

Left: When Thomas Hope had the historic and rather lovely Chart Park mansion razed in order to add its grounds and views to his personal Eden, one small part – half its sunken icehouse – escaped destruction. Half the roof remains.

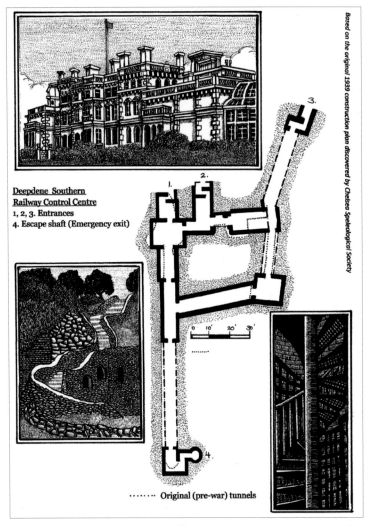

Deepdene Southern
Railway Control Centre
1, 2, 3. Entrances
4. Escape shaft (Emergency exit)

0 10' 20' 30'

·········· Original (pre-war) tunnels

Based on the original 1939 construction plan discovered by Chelsea Speleological Society

Plan of Deepdene's tunnels.

the River Thames. The casket was filled with water. An autopsy would prove nothing.

Deepdene House had once counted Disraeli and Winston Churchill as frequent visitors. Under Gregory it acquired a reputation as a destination where guests' marital status was less rigorously policed than at other establishments. While managed by Zhivotovsky's self-styled 'princess' of a daughter it was prosecuted for non-payment of its staff. She was found guilty of the false imprisonment of a servant. Her disastrous replacement was a boyishly young Italian waiter for whom the sybaritic Gregory had formed an attraction. With profits slipping, or more likely being squandered or embezzled away by this unlikely collection of exiles, fakers and spies, it all began to fall apart.

In 1934, Deepdene's once sylvan and peaceful grounds were scarred by an unpopular bypass built yards from the house. However, the rot had set in years before. There were rumours of illicit liaisons, blackmail, prostitution and meddling with the black arts that closely echoed the bestselling occult novels of Dennis Wheatley. A huge and locally-loathed neon sign was installed without permission atop the elegant roofline.

Its finances doomed, its staff unpaid, and its reputation mortally wounded by its association with the disgraced Gregory, the hotel was dying. A 1939 licensing inspection found just six guests.

Below: Deepdene's 85 foot (26 metre) long East Cave folly tunnel. Below right: During the residence at Deepdene of the Duchess of Marlborough, the tunnel was filled with all the statues whose nudity she disapproved of, making it a Medusa's cave for visiting younger family members. When the statuary was sold in 1917 it could not be exhibited in one Christie's auction room, lest its 30 ton weight collapsed the floor.

As a hotel Deepdene had no future, but as an emergency command centre relocated away from the likely bombing target of the metropolis, it did. In 1938, with war approaching, the house and grounds were taken over by Southern Railways.

It was a superb match of need and available resources. The building offered space, room for a 99 foot high radio mast, proximity to road and railway links and an array of subterranean real estate. Deepdene's second generation of underground glory was beginning.

Very little new excavation was necessary, apart from

Above left: Half of the tunnel was sheathed in a brick shield to strengthen it against bombs. The concrete path in the middle led to the shooting range targets. Above right: A formerly laddered, now dripping emergency exit shaft was bored into the tunnel roof. Left: 1790s graffito in the East Cave's end wall, surrounded by bullet holes and embedded lead bullet fragments.

the sinking of an emergency exit shaft protected at the surface by a shed-sized blockhouse with a pitched, bomb-deflecting roof. Construction mainly involved lining, strengthening (including the three entrances clustered around the 1770s Embattled Tower folly) and ventilation, plus the provision of a surface boiler room, toilet facilities and a huge concrete 'bomb burster' slab above the tunnels. Judging by contemporary photos, all built to a high standard. Work began before wartime shortages bit, so every effort was made to avoid the concrete bleakness, cold, darkness and damp that often characterised bunker living. Instead, the furnishings were comfortable, the ceilings high and the walls panelled and gloss-painted. The well-lit and business-like rooms barely looked like the interior of a shelter. Yet into them was fitted a telephone exchange, air plant, conference room, offices and accommodation, capable of 24 hour a day operation to plot damage, divert rolling stock, organise repairs and do everything necessary to maintain essential rail services throughout the worst of the Blitz and beyond. It is not wholly surprising that it was remembered as a happy place to work in those years.

Outside, the site became part of the Dorking anti-tank island, which saw the town expected to hold out against a mechanised German invasion force for one week, aided by an anti-armour ditch and hundreds of concrete dragon's teeth tank traps sited on the dene's banks.

The *Railway Gazette* lifted the veil on the formerly secret bunker operations in a well-illustrated factual article in 1945. As Andrew Emmerson and Tony Beard noted in *London's Secret Tubes*: 'The caves (described in the article) were in fact a magnificent 18th century shell-encrusted grotto of a calibre rivalling the more famous examples at Stourhead, Goodwood and Goldney.'

If the underground facilities were excellent, and still in partial use in the early

Above: Charles Howard's serpentine subterranean ramblings suddenly found a new life and purpose in WW2 as a communications and control bunker.
Right: The Embattled Tower folly is flanked by three sealed entrances to Howard's tunnels and the WW2 bunker.

Above: The main entrance tunnel. The other two entrances emerged into separate men's and women's toilet blocks protected by concrete roofs and by the Deepdene site's own anti-aircraft gun.
Left: The bunker was superbly equipped to carry out its work. With the help of this telephone exchange, the emergency working of the entire Southern Railways network could be directed.

Left: A switchboard equipment room adjoined the telephone exchange.
Below left: Within the room the main frame still stands guard.
Below right: Next to it was the battery room.

Left: Quietly rusting away within the bunker is an unmissable collection of surviving wartime electrical, communications and survival equipment.

Right: The former instrument room.
Far right: The night officer's room – now graffitied but once cosily furnished with a station-type clock, panelling, patterned flooring, two telephones, a desk and a nicely-made bed with tartan travelling rug atop it.

One of the bunker's current occupants, the large and (in adulthood) light-hating Cave Spider, which is among the UK's biggest arachnids.

Below: The control room: once panelled, where staff worked to oversee the vital Southern Railways network. Radiators kept them warm, radios kept them informed, and a system of ducting – clearly visible on the left – supplied them with fresh air. The doorway at the end leads to the meeting room.

1960s, what was happening above was not. The treatment of the mansion by Southern Railways and then British Rail was condemned by Nikolaus Pevsner and other architectural historians as a disgrace, closer to vandalism than negligence. Gregory and his gang had at least preserved the house. British Rail had been gifted a palace. It left it a wreck. By the time the railway company had moved on, Deepdene was rotting, and this irreplaceable architectural and historic gem was demolished in 1969.

Among the debris, in the palatial former home of some of the wealthiest and most treasure-rich men that England has ever known – as well as of a blackmailer through whose fat fingers many fortunes had trickled – a concealed room was found. It held a locked safe which the workmen rushed to break open. It was, of course, empty.

In the much reduced gardens, parts of which had been saved for public use, things were little better. The council had conserved the temple but, worried that vandalism might endanger visitors, they knocked it down. Similar concerns led to the mausoleum, which holds the remains of nine Hopes, being buried beneath concrete and earth in 1960. During the following decade, a modern office block, sensitively designed to nestle unobtrusively in the dene, was built on the site of the house. The *London Evening Standard* reported that: 'Two men escaped unhurt after being trapped behind a wall of flames when rubbish caught fire in a tunnel at Dorking today. The men, thought to be from a nearby building site, had clambered into the tunnel under Deepdene Avenue to explore.'

Below ground, everything was quiet. There was little decay; the communications equipment and telephone switchboard remained where they were, untouched in the darkness and rarely visited. A CSS report from 1978 recorded that the ice house, main shelter and World War Two-adapted East Cave, which had been used as a rifle range and had an escape shaft in its domed roof, were still extant. 'An approach to the caretakers,' it noted, 'can be productive'.

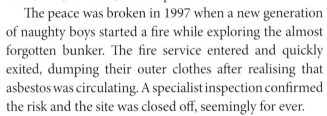

The peace was broken in 1997 when a new generation of naughty boys started a fire while exploring the almost forgotten bunker. The fire service entered and quickly exited, dumping their outer clothes after realising that asbestos was circulating. A specialist inspection confirmed the risk and the site was closed off, seemingly for ever.

However, the story doesn't end there. There are hopes that a grant can be secured to make the site safe and open it up the to the public in the same way as the South Street Caves.

Against all the odds, what remains of the gardens of 'Eden, Dorking' have already undergone an extraordinary renaissance. A joint coalition of a community group called The Friends of Deepdene, the Mausolea and Monuments Trust, Mole Valley District Council, Surrey Wildlife Trust and the travel firm Kuoni, which occupied the 1970s-built offices until 2018, has opened up some of the grounds to the public. They were triumphantly unveiled for the Heritage Open Days 2016.

The heart of the gardens now welcomes visitors, with regular tours on offer that include entry to the recently-exhumed mausoleum. The entrance to Charles Howard's collapsed hill-piercing tunnel is still there too. Converted into a small grotto, it later acquired ancient statuary and then a wartime front wall to make it suitable as a guardpost or office (probably not an ammunition store, as it had windows). It has now been artfully restored, sadly without the huge statue of an Egyptian god that originally graced the grotto. One niche remains unfinished, revealing the 17th century bricks and flints that cover the soft sandstone rockfall behind them which doomed the tunnel attempt.

Deepdene's surviving gardens have been brought back to life and the heavily contaminated surface buildings of wartime removed. However, one hazard remains: urban explorers who are prepared to force a way into the old bunker. Those who find it sealed and walk away deserve recognition but those who use pickaxes or power tools to break and enter, smashing doors, locks and historic walls in the process, leave openings behind them. They are aware of the asbestos danger. The children who

Above left: Looking down the exceptionally well-made emergency staircase, whose shaft was the tunnels' main air intake.
Above: The ventilator plant, which sucked air down the shaft and pumped it around the bunker. It could be sealed shut during a gas attack.

Above: Looking into one of the grilled air conduits
Right: The main tunnel led off from the ventilator room. Its large air ducting fed smaller conduits throughout the tunnels

stumble over their newly created entrances generally aren't.

In 2017, the bunker was entered at least twice in three weeks; those responsible left their filter masks and packaging strewn around. They cut the hazard tape placed to warn people of danger and dumped it, even though it would have taken a minute to move and then replace it. They also decided to use a section of rail to widen one of the openings created by earlier entrants. Like them, they ignored the effect of the rubble falling on the original 1930s emergency staircase and the fact that its handrail was cemented into the brickwork they had pulverised. The result was that a section of the stairs gave way, just leaving the handrail spiraling sadly and faithfully down into the pile of masonry and fallen metalwork below. A piece of World War Two history designed to survive the Blitz has fallen victim at least in part to people whose philosophy is said to be 'take nothing but photos, leave nothing but footprints'.

Under attack, the emergency exit building with an access hole smashed in it.

Despite this, Deepdene is rather magical. The parts that have been unearthed are fascinating. Those that have been left wild are just a tiny bit unearthly. Go off the paths, push under and through the trees and you still find ruins and rubble, dips and depressions, and hundreds of mossed dragons' teeth marching greenly over the heavily wooded hillside, whose dense canopy reaches down to claim them.

A similar story of reclamation is being written, on a smaller scale, at Betchworth Castle, which was once part of these same gardens. In 2011, historic buildings expert Martin Higgins bought the ruins for £1 from the local council, which in 1960 had come close to demolishing them on safety grounds, as they did the Deepdene temple. He is determined to conserve the ruins and improve their accessibility to the public.

Before it was deliberately ruined, the building was both a castle and not a castle: a fortified manor house dating back to 1379, possibly built on the site of an Iron Age hillfort, became a castle in law when the necessary licence was granted for it to be given battlements. In 1448, it was expanded and further castellated. Writing in his 1902 book *Picturesque Surrey*, when the building had been swallowed up as a garden feature for the Deepdene estate, author Gibson Thompson stated: 'Betchworth Park, which is part of the same domain, has one of the finest lime avenues in the world, leading to the shapeless ruins of Betchworth Castle, which was originally fortified and embattled in 1449 by Abraham Tucker, who wrote his metaphysical "Light of Nature Pursued," and died, here. The last volumes of this scholarly work were written, after he had become blind, with the aid of a machine which he invented to guide his hand and enable him to write legibly.'

That structure was reduced in size in the 1690s, only to be reborn in the 1790s with new additions designed by the great neo-classical architect, Royal Academician, art collector, bricklayer's son and knight of the realm, Sir John Soane.

Above: Seventy-nine emergency stairs used to lead from within the bunker to the surface.
Left: Hundreds of dragon's teeth stud the dene's slopes.

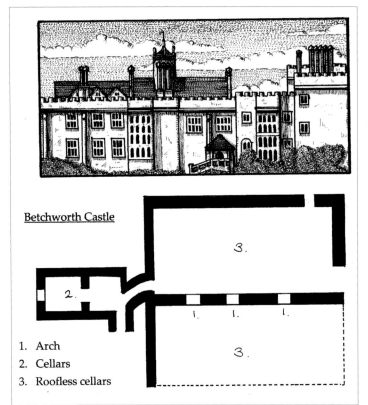

Betchworth Castle

1. Arch
2. Cellars
3. Roofless cellars

Above: Betchworth Castle.

Below: Inside one of the three former sets of cellars. The arches on the left led to further de-ceilinged cellars. Below right: On the other side of that three-arched wall: more cellars left roofless and exposed in order to make picturesque ruins.

Unfortunately, crisp neo-classicism wasn't what Deepdene's land-greedy Henry Hope was looking for when he bought it in 1835. Like his father, Hope unashamedly demolished any historic and serviceable stately home whose grounds he added to his own, irrespective of the social and economic consequences. Even the staidly Victorian Charles Rose came dangerously near to criticising the gentry when he hinted at the opposition caused by this latest example of the Hopes' mania for acquiring and destroying estates: 'The remains of this fine old residence, once the busy scene of human life, became silent and solitary, the haunt of owls, and the nesting place of other birds. The third demolition of a mansion on the Deepdene estate – one having once stood in Chart Park, and another on the site of the present Deepdene Gardens – produced, as in the two previous instances, much regret among the inhabitants.'

At Betchworth, Hope opted for partial demolition, so that the remains could serve as that most desirable folly and prospect improver, a castle in ruins. Whether he succeeded is a matter of personal taste. Left alone, the building would have aged into its role. Arguably, the attempt to force the change deprived it of the magic of either a true ruined castle or a well made fake one. The castle had very substantial working cellars, with those beneath the medieval tower dating back to the 15th century. Unusually, almost all of them were opened to the air and then part-filled to enhance the mood of age and desolation. Only the two smallest, oldest (and perhaps most dungeonlike) escaped being prised open and made naked to the onlooker's eye. Their future, like that of the rest of the structure, is now assured.

If Deepdene's gardens were, in their time, a true Eden, then they were rivalled by those at the home of their visitor and admirer, the hugely wealthy landowner John

Left: Twin entrances to the oldest, and still roofed, cellars.
Below, left to right: Cellars below the medieval tower, whose walls, owner Martin Higgins believes, date from around 1448, were externally remodelled around 1705 and then revaulted in brick in 1798 to accommodate drains improved by Sir John Soane. The second chamber of the oldest cellars. The aperture at the end would once have looked up into another cellar. Surviving castle masonry found in the second chamber.

Evelyn. The gardens of his 17th century family home, Wotton House, are simply extraordinary. Unlike Deepdene, both they and the mansion that they surrounded are still with us, under the custodianship of the De Vere Wotton Park Hotel. What Evelyn started his family continued, creating a Xanadu of temples and terraces, groves and grottoes, cataracts and canals, crossed by countless bridges. The family's pleasure grounds also included a kangaroo meadow and a tortoise house (probably actually for turtles or terrapins) complete with swimming pond. (Built in the style of a Greek temple, naturally.) Of course, if you have a tortoise temple you'll want to show it off to your friends, so at the rear it has a wide stone staircase to a rooftop viewing terrace. All this was set in a walled garden big enough to hold a dozen farm cottages. It was built between 1820 and 1830, a time of rural unemployment, poverty and homelessness, when farm labourers fought against starvation and exploitation with arson, sabotage and protest. One hundred and fourteen special constables were armed and sworn in. The cavalry were let loose on the demonstrators. Dorking erupted into a riot. The wonder is that there weren't more of them.

Right: Wotton House.

Right: Remaining wall of one grotto.
Far right: Narrow carved stone passages connect behind and above the temple, producing a natural cooling effect for its visitors.
Below: The garden temple.

Left: Alone in the woods, buried in the hillside where the 1870 Ordnance Survey map says it should be: Wotton House's icehouse. Above: Inside the egg-shaped icehouse. The water-stained brickwork shows where blocks of ice would have been stored

*Above left: The tortoise house.
Above: The extraordinary Wotton House has two grottoes.
Left: Inside the grotto.*

CHAPTER THREE

Digging for victory

One of the obvious routes for an invasion of Britain is a landing on the south coast of England, followed by a sweep northwards into Surrey. This means passing through the funnel of the Dorking Gap, the break in the highly defensible North Downs created by the valley of the River Mole. For centuries the nation used a 'fleet, fort, field' strategy to resist and deter aggression. This relied on the Royal Navy, backed by coastal fortresses, and only lastly on a small army supplemented by a militia. By the 19th century warfare was changing. Concerns about the expansionist intent of France led in the 1860s to the building of Britain's equivalent of the Maginot Line, a massive peacetime construction programme of expensive and technically advanced fortresses and sea forts that became known (probably unfairly, given their possible deterrent effect) as 'Palmerston's follies'.

In 1870, everything changed. The unexpected and almost unthinkable Prussian defeat of continental superpower France, grown fat on a hubristic belief in its own military and intellectual superiority, ushered in a new era of warfare. The threat found its voice in the 1871 novella *The Battle of Dorking*, by a Royal Engineers captain called George Tomkyns Chesney. It told the story of an attack by a Germanic power whose army advances on London from the coast. The decision is taken to halt the invaders at the North Downs, 'the line of the great chalk-range'. The story's narrator is a member of the Volunteers, the auxiliary regiments intended to supplement the regular army, which is fatally overstretched defending Britain's imperial possessions. It is clear where the enemy will try to bypass the natural defences of the Downs, so he is sent to 'the little town of Dorking, nestling in the trees'. There, on Denbies hillside and Box Hill, the British Empire meets its end, as the brave but muddled territorials and the efficient but too few regular army soldiers are outflanked by an army that ensures that its men, unlike the storyteller's fellows, get the rations, trenchcoats and ammunition they need, when they need them.

The book succeeded brilliantly in persuading the public that imperial Britain might be unready for warfare in the age of the telegraph, troop movement by railway, and advances in artillery. It also singlehandedly invented the genre of invasion literature, giving birth to similarly influential books such as *The Riddle of the Sands*, *When William Came* and, arguably, *The War of the Worlds*.

The story was an international success, and led to increasing calls in the 1880s and 90s for the construction of a line of fortresses to protect London. These grew in the face of a resurgent France, whose Minister of Marine, Admiral Aube, promised that 'the day is coming when Britain's shores will be assaulted and her ports burnt by the fleet of a victorious enemy'. In Dorking, Lord Ashcombe paid £1,500 to build a Volunteer Drill Hall in West Street. In London, the decision was taken to equip the North Downs with a number of blockhouses that would hold ammunition, tools and barbed wire ready for use to build a 72 mile long line of entrenchments. Their placing was like a checklist from Chesney's story, including Box Hill, Denbies, Betchworth,

Reigate and Guildford. These were not the huge fortresses of the Palmerston era, but much more modest tokens of a new and vastly cheaper approach: a mix of mobilisation centres and very undersized forts. Historian Victor Smith concisely summed them up as combining 'limited permanent construction with contingency planning for a shielding arc of fieldworks to create a vast entrenched camp'. Rather quaintly, each unmanned centre was guarded only by a caretaker, who had a cottage alongside the tool store. (These cottages were all quickly sold off. Box Hill's became the Fort Tearoom, and, for several years, a Wimpy bar.)

The mobilisation centres have long been mislabelled as forts. They weren't. They were depots whose surface rooms could assume the role of a strongpoint. Their role was to hold ammunition, shovels, picks and wheelbarrows. Despite their ramparts and firing steps, the function of redoubt was a secondary one. The real defence was to be done from positions dug between and in front of them.

Despite this and their complete lack of armament, at very little financial cost the defences wove a spell of supposed readiness and fighting fitness. Rarely has deterrent propaganda come so cheaply. Gibson Thompson was typical of public opinion when, in his 1902 book *Picturesque Surrey*, he erroneously stated that Dorking was made famous by Chesney's story, 'but that was in 1871, before Box Hill was crowned by a fort armed with heavy guns'.

At the Box Hill centre the surface buildings were half sunk into the sheltering earth, helping to disguise their outlines and protect them from artillery fire. The interior casemate rooms were beautifully finished in brick, each with a large armour plate exterior door, and each capable of serving as a last ditch fighting point. However, it was in the layer below that the centre's real work was to be done. Down there are the magazines, the all-important subterranean chambers where shell, shot and powder were to be kept ready to be fused and armed. They were maintained under the latest, strictest and most scientific conditions, to prevent the whole place and all in it being blow off the earth's surface. The safety rules weren't just rigidly enforced, they were built into the very fabric of the fort, and even into the clothes the troops wore. Soldiers entering the central magazine room had to replace their hobnailed boots with leather slippers. They needed to change from their uniforms into special colour-coded cotton clothing, with wooden, not metal buttons, in case the cloth harboured a pebble or speck of grit that might strike a spark. A benched area with wooden barriers, known as the shifting lobby, reminded them that they dare go no further without making the changes. For safe working, light was needed but it couldn't be allowed near the

Below left: Half sunk into the protective landscape: Box Hill mobilisation centre. Below right: The 'fort' redoubt, with its magazines buried below it

explosives. The solution is found across Britain's 19th century fortifications: windows set into the magazines with armoured glass covers. In these recesses, candle lamps could be placed but only from the outside entry corridor and from a special, narrow lamp tunnel behind the magazine rooms.

Almost as soon as they were finished the defence line's buildings were decreed redundant and sold off. The military situation had changed again: Britain and France were making up and the Royal Navy was resurgent, its new dreadnoughts the masters of the oceans. In 1909 Eric Parker, the author of a walking guide to Surrey, reported from Box Hill that 'The wisdom of a War Office cleared a wide space of trees and built a fort there; the wisdom of another War Office abandoned the fort as useless. There it remains, behind spiked railings, the idlest monument of a whim'.

Top row and above left: Inside the semi-buried surface buildings. Each half-buried casemate had doorways and windows guarded by loopholed armour plate.
Above: One of two entrances, each of which gave onto a guardroom/ lamproom and the stairs down.

Far left: The stairs to the underground magazine level with, on the right, the entrance to the tight little lamp tunnel.
Left: Each lamp window had two panes of strengthened glass; only the one on the safe side could be opened. Guard rails held the lamp in place. An air inlet is visible on the left, as is a square-cut chimney above.

In the end the Box Hill mobilisation centre, like its siblings, never experienced combat. In the world wars it saw limited use for troop accommodation and storage. But it was the wrong design in the wrong place in the wrong time when it was most desperately needed. In 1940 after Dunkirk and the fall of France what was the point of a place to store artillery supplies when, with invasion imminent, there was no artillery to store?

When visiting Box Hill Fort as a child in the 1960s and 70s it was possible to climb over the rubbish and the fallen armoured shutters (which remarkably weren't stolen for scrap), descend the rubble-choked stairs and explore the pitch black underground magazines. It's a curious fact that such adventures were lit by quickly dying spills of newspaper, since in the 1960s it was somehow much easier for a small boy to borrow matches than a torch. As each burning page died, you quickly used it to light another and looked for those discarded by others to get you further in (and back out again).

Left: The narrow tunnel that serviced the lamps.
Below: Underground corridor, studded with lamp apertures, and with entries to the three magazine rooms. In the first is a large water tank. At the passage's end is a second set of stairs up. The supports for the shifting lobby barrier flank the middle doorway.

In the next decade the fort was fenced off and later housed sheep. Its outside has now been nicely spruced up by the National Trust, and the shutters are back in place. Since its 1904 closure, despite all the fences and alternating periods of openness and then being locked, there is likely to have been one class of continuing visitor: bats. The interior is now locked and given over to them, and thanks are due to the Surrey Bat Group for allowing entry during one of their inspections, which revealed that the rare Barbastelle bat is now among those roosting there.

Above: The central and most dangerous magazine, guarded by a shifting lobby with wooden barriers. The support for one of these can be seen to the left of the doorway.

Box Hill mobilisation centre

1. Lamp passage
2. Main passage
3. Lamp window
4. Shell store
5. Central magazine
6. Shifting lobby entrance
7. Gutter

1. Bren embrasure
2. Spent cartridge trap
3. Tripod support
4. Internal blast wall
5. Rifle embrasure
6. Six-pounder embrasure
7. Six-pounder holdfast

Box Hill pillboxes

Left: Plans of Box Hill mobilisation centre and pillboxes.

CHAPTER FOUR

Defence in depth

War transforms humanity into its cave-dwelling ancestors. Throughout history its approach has heralded an orgy of burying food and valuables, the digging of hiding places and the construction of fortifications, sally ports and escape tunnels. The world wars of the 20th century, with their threat of death from above, added a new impetus and scientific method to this flight below, an atavistic need to burrow and wrap ourselves in soil, stone and concrete.

War democratises the underground. Suddenly it is no longer only cellarmen and servants, miners and labourers who occupy it, leaving their carved names behind. When the brass bands play and feet begin to pound, we go underground.

The Second World War was a total war. Everyone was affected. This was not like the later Cold War, with its secrecy and covert bunker building. This was hot. This was visible. This was everywhere. The town's geography changed. Steel girders were implanted in key roads to stop tanks. Concrete cylinders squatted in groups ready to be rolled into place to back them up. Ugly square mini bunkers, just big enough for a desk, kettle and chairs, appeared all over the town. Nicknamed 'the pillboxes' by locals, they provided protection for ARP (Air Raid Precautions) wardens who had to stay on duty on the surface during bombing. 'Dragons' teeth' were sown along the railway embankments. Lights were cloaked. Enamel shelter signs were planted, pointing to public refuges. Pillboxes and sandbagged machine gun nests flanked the main roads and peppered the hillsides. Road, rail and river blocks sprang up everywhere. The Mole itself was strengthened, fortified and made sheer-sided. A great anti-tank ditch was dug between the limeworks and Box Hill.

Some of that geography remains on The Nower, moss covered, grass grown, demolished, crunching underfoot and split by trees. There are clay water pipes, an old stove in the bracken, with Home Guard leggings discarded by it, broken NAAFI teacups, rusted posts for holding barbed wire, a broken stirrup pump, galvanised water tanks and big unexplained hummocks squatting among the trees which, below the earth and grass that cover them, prove to be dumps of broken concrete, twisted metal, sheets of corrugated iron and asbestos.

Far left: The Nower is dotted with the detritus of World War Two.
Left: The characteristic footprints of three Nissen huts.

Here the Home Guard paraded and patrolled, and the British and Canadian armies made ready for two invasions – first to help defend against the expected German one, and then, four years later, to train for the liberation of the Continent. At first they lived in billets and tents, in an environment defensively laced with barbed wire, but later an encampment was built and a training ground created. Nissen huts sprouted everywhere, intricate trench networks were dug, a wide mud-filled ditch that had to be swung across on ropes was sunk, and a wall was built to scramble over in full kit and carrying a rifle. Half filled or sunken under the earth, they're still there.

Local resident John Molyneux recalled: 'The Nower wasn't out of bounds, unlike the Second Nower, which became a training area. My father had a permit allowing access to most parts. He used to take me for walks and often I accompanied him when he was delivering to the farms. The Second Nower was part of the Bury Hill estate and contained a small pistol range, a warren of trenches, several scaling walls and the drive was lined with Nissen huts. In a nearby field were two old tanks, filled with concrete, which the soldiers attempted to destroy with mortar bombs.'

Despite plans to demolish them, the 29 Nissen huts lived on after the war as housing for people who had lost their homes to bombing raids. This only officially ceased in 1950, leaving the buildings as a derelict and excitingly dangerous playground. It's clear that on their demolition much of their fabric was simply dumped nearby and given a light covering of earth. Cement, brickwork and their distinctive overgrown oblong footprints remain within the woods.

The trenches were almost lost when rubble from bomb-damaged buildings was dumped in them, but lines of diggings remain, slowly becoming shallower as their sides crumble and they fill with trees and generations of fallen leaves.

They were placed there not only to teach how to dig trenches, but also how to storm them. Hidden among them is a buried bunker that would probably have been used during live firing exercises. Virtually invisible now, its existence is only revealed by a few traces of brick and concrete. It appears that the stairway down was deliberately blocked by collapsing its ceiling, making it impossible to enter without using an excavator. Like the trenches, it remains as a trace of that great endeavour to end the Nazi domination of Europe. It is humbling to think how many young men struggled and sweated here to learn the skills that might mean life or death across the Channel and then to wonder how many of them did, or did not, make it home in the end.

Nissen huts, machine gun emplacements and encampments once also clustered on Box Hill and, out of the way, half hidden, largely unrecognised and overgrown,

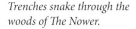

Trenches snake through the woods of The Nower.

the traces of some of them remain. However, the best known defensive position there is the one built for the war that never came: Box Hill Fort. As mentioned, it had sister centres. One at Betchworth and one at Denbies (demolished in the 1970s and a bungalow built on top), where in World War Two the Home Guard training school was relocated from London's Osterley Park. This was in part to neutralise the political plans of its influential Marxist co-founder, the Spanish Civil War veteran, serial philanderer and born publicist Tom Wintringham. A highly effective public champion of the Home Guard, his aim was to forge it into a people's guerilla army. Relocated to Dorking he began teaching anti-tank warfare, unaware that he was as guilty as the generals he accused of fighting the last war – in his case the Spanish conflict. His suggested tactics (stopping an armoured column by placing soup plates on the road to simulate mines, then removing the tank's tracks by jamming in a crowbar or wooden batten) might have been suitable in extremis for confronting the tiny, two man Italian tankettes or lightweight Panzer Is he had seen in Spain; they would have been suicidal against a German invasion force.

The Home Guard school was a major national undertaking, run by Major Hugh Pollock (husband of Enid Blyton) which brought together a singular but effective mix of Regular Army soldiers, Spanish Civil War combatants, artists and intellectuals. Another influential instructor was local resident and journalist John Langdon-Davies, conscientious objector turned author of *The Home Guard Fieldcraft Manual*.

Above left: One of the training trenches with behind it, a practice climbing wall.
Above: Now almost completely invisible, a blocked bunker entrance.

Langdon-Davies co-founded the charity that is now Plan International, in response to a plea from a Spanish Republican father that read: 'This is José. I am his father. When Santander falls I will be shot. Please, whoever finds my son take care of him for me.'

Denbies, like so much of the countryside surrounding the town, was also an important Canadian Army assembly and training area. At least three armoured vehicles were buried there in 1944, probably by pushing them into the anti-tank ditch. Two have been recovered: they were both

Recovered in 2017, the second Covenanter tank dug up at Denbies.

Covenanters, a cruiser tank rightly decreed insufficiently armed and armoured for combat. Despite this, 1,700 of them were inexplicably built during and after the desperate post-Dunkirk period. They were quickly relegated to the training and range target roles. The first Denbies Covenanter was disinterred in 1983, still with petrol in the tank and

As combat tanks Covenanters were useless, but they were beautifully made. Controls, ammunition stowage and markings are all identifiable despite being buried underground for 73 years.

its painted unit markings visible. Superbly restored, it now graces Bovington Tank Museum.

When the British Expeditionary Force retreated from Dunkirk in June 1940, it left behind all its best equipment: 11,000 Bren and Vickers machine guns, nearly 700 tanks and 1,000 carriers, 65,000 wheeled vehicles, around 500 anti-aircraft guns, most of its heavy artillery and 821 vital anti-tank guns. This left just 170 of the latter back in Britain to resist the imminent invasion.

The situation was utterly desperate. Every kind of antique and improvised weapon was dug out and pressed into use. This was the time when the Home Guard were issued with pikes and pepper to throw in the eyes of German troops. When Winston Churchill visited the coastline at Dover, which was certain to be the invaders' chosen landing ground, he found the entire five mile stretch defended by just three anti-tank guns, each with only six rounds. France's Marshal Philippe Pétain probably summed up the opinion of many, not least his French War Cabinet colleagues, when he allegedly commented, not without satisfaction, that within weeks Britain would have its neck wrung like a chicken's. Faced with an existential shortage of steel, artillery, tanks and anti-tank weapons, Britain substituted concrete for metal. If panzers could not be destroyed at a distance by anti-tank guns, then they must be halted long enough for the job to be done up close and by hand. The German armoured columns would have to be delayed, allowing mobile reserves to be brought up to confront them. Designated towns and villages would need to become nodal 'islands' holding out alone against all odds. Panzers would have to be fought with petrol bombs and satchel charges. That meant obstacles and roadblocks, every one of which had to be an ambush point if the famously efficient German combat engineers were not to instantly clear it away. The strategy, known as 'defence in depth', demanded anti-tank barriers: ditches, rivers, girders and hundreds of thousands of concrete cubes, blocks, cylinders and pyramids, all guarded by gunpits or half-buried pillboxes. These were camouflaged or disguised and placed in pairs or groups, so that each could support the other. In front of them there would be barbed wire, often mines, and always a trench or trenches, which would only be left by its defenders in favour of the pillbox itself at the last minute.

Of the seven or more pillboxes built in Dorking, two fine examples survive on Box Hill. One is near the Stepping Stones. These had been removed so as not to aid the enemy, though it's hard to imagine how their loss would dramatically slow down an invading force well capable of wading across the ancient ford without them. (The concrete hardstanding in the nearby car park in what a wartime map calls Dead Man's

Lane was put in place by Canadian troops, who waterproofed their vehicles there, then drove them into the river to test them).

One of the pair of pillboxes is literally built into the hillside and would have overlooked Dorking's mile long anti-tank ditch, whose Mole end was marked by a riverblock made from steel cables and concrete pipes, many of which remain today. This strongpoint was constructed to hold an aged six-pounder naval cannon. Dating back to 1885, declared outdated in the face of armoured dreadnoughts, these had been withdrawn from service in Edwardian times. They were pulled from retirement in order to arm British tanks in World War One. Long obsolete, the mothballed reserves were hurriedly raided again in 1940 to equip pillboxes, despite a shortage of ammunition for them. Of course, there weren't enough of them to actually go around. The highly optimistic plan was that they would be moved to the danger areas at the last minute, despite being under aerial attack and on roads choked with advancing troops and fleeing civilians.

Further upriver, and guarding 12 massive anti-tank cylinders, is a hexagonal Type FW3/24 shellproof model. This was about as good as British pillboxes got, much stronger and more heavily

armed than the ordinary Type 24, reflecting the strategic importance of its position. Made massively thick to resist shells, it was part sunk into the earth to lower its profile. Every embrasure was pre-manufactured to house a Bren light machine gun on a tripod mount. An internal wall would reduce the risk of any bullets that did enter passing through and killing the defender opposite, or ricocheting around inside. The only odd omission in the Box Hill example is that the usual backwards-facing embrasures have not been included. Perhaps the authorities envisaged that it might be possible to retreat from this pillbox, an option not available to the crew of the anti-tank one: once they were in, they were in till the end. Their only escape would involve either climbing

The Stepping Stones with, at right, the steps where military vehicles were driven into the river to test their waterproofing.

Left, clockwise from top left: Still buried in the slopes of Box Hill, a pillbox that guarded the Mole Gap and the end of the now-filled anti-tank ditch that ran from the Dorking limeworks. Inside. Slowly filling with earth, and too low to stand up in. The thickness of the walls is shown by the rifle loophole in the left hand wall. Gunner's eye view, showing the holdfast to which the (probably 19th century) six-pounder gun would have been bolted. Below the pillbox: concrete cylinders emplaced to complement the anti-tank ditch and prevent vehicles fording the River Mole. And their hengelike brothers on the opposite bank. They would have all been linked by steel hawsers to make a significant obstacle to tanks (or boats).

Top left: An invader's view of the strengthened Type 24 infantry pillbox.

Top right: Looking in from outside, showing the sheer size of the internal blast wall, which displays, like its neighbour, a possible maker's mark – a tree within a triangle.

Above left: The mount and the spent cartridge trap show that all the embrasures were designed to hold Bren guns mounted on tripods – making them capable of indirect fire on the river block, even if the enemy put up a smokescreen to cover a river crossing.

Above right: Still standing sentry on the riverbank, a row of 12 huge anti-tank cylinders.

up a nearly sheer slope in full view of the enemy, or skidding down it into their arms.

The Type 24 shellproof pillbox would have given some protection from flanking attack to its cannon-mounting comrade but the fact that it might fail was obviously considered, as shown by the addition of a rifleman's position to the left of the six-pounder mount. The brick interior and exterior is deceptive. Because of the massive building programme to construct 28,000 pillboxes nationwide, there was a shortage of wooden panels for the shuttering in which to pour concrete. Brick was an effective alternative. In the Type 24 shellproof, corrugated iron sheeting was used, giving it a distinctive and slightly futuristic look.

Dorking has endured disease, civil war, famine and riot but its people have rarerly been in greater peril than in World War Two. The danger was foreseen. The need to take (literally) concrete action against it, apparently, was not. The foundations were there: the January 1938 ARP Act laid the groundwork for a civil defence organisation and meant that even before the war began, gasmasks were being distributed and school air raid shelters built. The popular will was there too, as proved by the multitude of volunteers for the support and emergency services. Everybody knew that the first great threat would come from the air, in the shape of an expected rain of poison gas, high explosives and incendiary bombs. They knew too that Dorking's population would need protection. Yet the story of the town's shelter provision is one of good intentions held back by parsimony and shortsightedness.

Right: Two of the pillbox's embrasures, with the massive internal blast wall to the right.

It's probably not unfair to sum up the history of Dorking's civil defence as one of a population wanting decent and, in its eyes, easily-dug protection underground, while the council, from its Pippbrook base, insisted instead on cheap surface shelters and then, with the Blitz well under way and the danger at its peak, converted cellars.

A full twenty months before hostilities began, the vicar of St Paul's was rather idealistically urging the digging of a public tube shelter right along the High Street. In April 1939, the *Dorking Advertiser* reported that: 'A section of the Dorking public has been urging that shelters be constructed in the hills of Cotmandene and the Nower, and the High Street caves be used.' The newspaper had already reflected the common view that 'Dorking had miles of underground tunnelling which could be adapted into shelters'. The suggestion was swatted away by the council, which stated that 'The Government, advised by experts and having full knowledge of the likelihood of bombs and of the possibilities of protection, have not given support to the construction of deep shelters'.

With just five days to go before war was declared, the chairman of the Dorking Urban Council Ratepayers' Association was reported as declaring 'We have had more advice than we wanted'. The council, he said, 'had no intention or desire to provide shelters for every person, just those caught in the streets'.

A year later, as the first bombs fell on the town and the Battle of Britain raged above it, the position was little better, with nothing to show but hopelessly inadequate surface shelters placed near shops and the less than overwhelming announcement that the shelters at St Paul's and St Joseph's schools would be opened to the general public outside school hours.

An attempt to boost morale was reported in November 1940. In a council meeting the chairman of the ARP Committee gave 'a reassuring statement about air raid shelters'. Up to seven weeks before, he said, provision had been only for shelters in shopping areas. Then, the government changed its mind and gave Dorking permission to build communal street ones. 'Within days', he claimed, seventeen more street shelters had been started. 'The committee had received scores of letters about shelters – some constructive, some few hopelessly unpractical and a small number ludicrous.' In reality, the situation was profoundly unsatisfactory. The surface shelters were tiny, completely inadequate and behind schedule. Three cellars had been assigned to shelter use but lacked bunks and toilets. Too late, the search began for alternatives, including a tardy attempt to survey the borough's multitude of 'natural caves' and tunnels for their suitability.

Three months later, little had been achieved: 'The Surveyor reported to the A.R.P. Committee that he had inspected a considerable number of caves in Dorking. With one exception, he considered them to be unsuitable for adaptation. The exception was the cave at the rear of the premises of Messrs. B. Turner, Ltd, in the High Street …The Surveyor presented plans for the adaptation at a cost of about £750. The cave would accommodate 420 persons.' Miss Evans (Councillor) doubted whether anyone would venture in, as, according to her, 'it was a most eerie place'. She was assured that it would be different when it had electric light, seating, roof supports and some flooring.

Time was wasted as everyone in authority agreed that the cellar of the Star and Garter Hotel (now the Lincoln Arms) would make a perfect shelter and immediate action was authorised. Within weeks that decision had been reversed. The surveyor assured the councillors that work was going ahead to adapt basements at Bembridge House in West Street, Milton Motors in the High Street, and the Dorking Book Shop in South Street. He added that 150 steel bunks were being bought. A contract to add wooden seating to the seventeen communal shelters at a cost of £3 10s each was approved. However, Mr Wilkinson, the ARP Committee chairman, pointed out that, 'If a person has the average length legs, it will be impossible for him to sit in the wretched things.' He described the construction of the surface shelters as 'scandalous' and a 'waste of money'. He was right. A photo of one outside the Gun pub in North Street shows that it was like a small bus shelter made of brieze blocks. The whole thing was no deeper than the narrow pavement, making it cramped, vulnerable and impossible to sit down in even if there had been a bench.

The council was quick to shift the blame onto central government. The surveyor reported that tunnelling was 'impracticable' due to the stringent requirements of a Home Security circular. No one was convinced. In Reigate the council converted sand mines into shelters for schools and the public; one of them is still helping draw over 2,500 visitors to the town during just five days each year as part of the excellent tunnel open days run there. In Guildford, the council drove a shelter for 1,000 people into the side of Foxenden Quarry. Surrey County Council dug four impressive shelters, each capable of holding up to 1,500 people, near railway stations (making them suitable for residents but also people fleeing London) at Epsom, Epsom Downs, Coulsdon and Kenley. Another at Banstead was abandoned when the dug chalk was found to be too soft to give the expected protection.[1]

In Dorking there was no hiding the inadequacy of what had been provided. Public opinion decried the surface shelters: they were too small, too wet, too cramped, too cold and simply unsafe.

As the late-arriving, converted basement shelters began to come into use, there were calls for seating, lavatories and heating to be installed. In August 1941, a first aid post was opened in the basement at Pippbrook but it was later reported that, like the shelters, it was too cold to sit or work in. The owners of some shops asked if they could add electric sockets to the refuges below their premises, so that people could brew a cup of hot tea.

This dissatisfaction found expression in vandalism, with the surface shelters a particular target. In January 1942 the *Dorking Advertiser* reported that shelters would be kept locked when not in use. A year later it noted that: 'Seats have been broken and lightbulbs have been smashed or stolen … Somewhen, one of the marauders will be caught and he will be, we hope, heavily punished.' In a newspaper that was by then mainly full of items on pigswill, firewatching, salvage drives and Aid to Russia, the controversy over shelters never went away. As early as 1940, the paper had declared: 'Strange how the Dorking Urban District Council resent even the slightest suggestion of criticism. Dorking's slogan should be "Pippbrook is always right".' The continuing, heated and open debate over shelters is a tribute both to the role of local newspapers in examining authority and to the democratic rights that the war was in part being fought to defend.

---

[1] To test the efficacy of the designs, at Epsom Downs a 550 pound bomb was sunk 23 and a half feet (7.2 metres) into the chalk – the depth it could be expected to penetrate if dropped in a raid – directly above one of the shelter tunnels, which was filled with measuring instruments and cages full of mice and canaries. It was then detonated. The tunnels held and the test subjects survived.

So what has become of the many surface shelters placed alongside or behind shops that were once household names in the town? There was one at Chitty's butchers and slaughterhouse, another at Jay's ('Everything for the garden'), two behind Dunn's the furrier and skin merchant and two behind Grice's the bakers and confectioners. All gone now. As have most of those shops, a reminder of the cull of historic buildings in the town that continued throughout the 20th century. Cottages, streets and alleys, of such ancient picturesqueness that even in Victorian times they were attracting photographers and artists to Dorking, were all levelled.

The fact that the multitude of surface shelters were removed without leaving any trace illustrates why they inspired so little confidence. (Compare their removal to how difficult it was to destroy pillboxes). Also now gone without trace are the ARP posts that once dotted the town.

And the underground basement shelters? What remains of the refuge for 140 people at the Methodist Church in South Street? Or those below Baron's Garage and Baker's Garage (worrying choices given the proximity of fuel tanks), Messrs B Turner, Ltd, 'purveyors of Locally Fed Home-killed Meat', the Dorking Book Shop, or Quick's, the well-known wireless and cycle stores, with Maison Marcelle, 'specialists in permanent waving' above it?

Those strengthened basements would have offered more comfort and safety than the unpopular surface ones but, almost without exception, they're all gone too, the shops, garages and church that hosted them wiped away for car parks, modern developments, St Martin's Walk and Waitrose. One thing is known about them, evident from the official meetings that spawned them: that cheaper was clearly better. The council was delighted when the Methodist Church in South Street requested no funds for making its cellars into a shelter or when the owner of The Garth on Horsham Road offered an outbuilding suitable for protecting 80 people. Apparently, its adaptation 'would cost £10'. This was an unbelievable figure, when even the materials for each of the little concrete block ARP posts cost £80. The gold standard of tunnelled shelters had been rejected. What was offered instead was a mix of damp, toiletless, tiny surface shelters and strengthened basements. (The latter were not necessarily ineffective, but only so long as the strengthening really took place.)

An answer to that question can be found at 294 High Street, which appears to be one of the town's last two survivors of this type of shelter. In 1939, this imposingly solid Victorian building was home to a garage called Milton Motors. The council surveyor's eyes must have

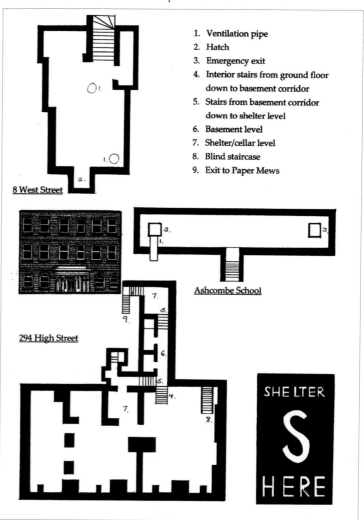

1. Ventilation pipe
2. Hatch
3. Emergency exit
4. Interior stairs from ground floor down to basement corridor
5. Stairs from basement corridor down to shelter level
6. Basement level
7. Shelter/cellar level
8. Blind staircase
9. Exit to Paper Mews

8 West Street

Ashcombe School

294 High Street

SHELTER
S
HERE

Left to right: The entrance in Paper Mews to the shelter at 294 High Street, complete with concrete cap, steps and door lintel.
The doorway opens into a basement that communicates by sunken corridor with the main cellar area. Leading off the passage are stairs down to the shelter (left) and a short corridor that has been given a massive concrete base (centre).
Electrical starter switch for now disappeared plant.

lit up when he saw the cellars. They are huge, as big as the whole building above, which is supported on a mass of trust-inspiring below-ground pillars. There is easily enough space for 150 people. A convenient alley at the side from which the public could enter via concrete steps is still visible today in Paper Mews. There was also an interior cellar staircase which would provide an emergency exit. True, the ceilings are a little bit low: anyone of six foot or over would have to stoop just a little. Otherwise, this would make a perfect shelter.

Well, almost perfect. There's a quick visual test to determine whether something was built as a cellar or an air raid shelter. If you can see the floorboards and joists, then it's the former. This one fails the test. Rather shockingly, the ceiling has not been reinforced. This matters because the whole building might collapse into the cellar if there was a near miss and, even more seriously, because any bomb that pierced the roof and floors above and wasn't stopped by the usual concrete ceiling given to a shelter would be likely to explode in the crowded shelter itself. The lack of reinforcement would have turned it from a refuge into a deathtrap.

Perhaps this particular shelter was rushed into service. It is to be hoped that the same mistake was not allowed to happen in the others in the town, even though another proposed basement shelter in West Street remained similarly unprotected.

Right: The house's original double cellars are huge and well supported by solid brick pillars.

Far left: The addition of two brick walls created twin cubicle spaces.
Left: The second shelter chamber, once a separate cellar, that has been accessed by smashing through the wall to create a doorway (left of picture).

At No.294, some alteration has taken place but it is difficult to say whether this was for the garage or for public protection. A plinth-like mass of concrete three and a half feet (1 metre) high has been added to one whole section that has been created by installing a brieze block wall. From it concrete stairs descend into what looks like a further level but is just a void that would have held machinery or cabling, very possibly the ventilation plant. Some iron girders have been added in places, but when is uncertain. The same applies to the concrete that covers what would originally have been a stone floor.

A shelter like this would once have been dark and muggy, full of humanity dying for a fag, frightened, wondering when they could surface again and whether they could hold off going to the bucket toilets whose smell would become more and more awful as the air raid continued. It's difficult to recapture that feeling here. For years now the premises above have been used for takeaway food sales and the plentiful basement space and corridors are swept and painted. It is no longer possible to find the shelterers' graffiti, warning notices, old fittings and signs that you always hope to discover in any disused shelter.

Only one other public basement shelter still appears to exist: Montague Burton's. In 1938 the famous gentlemen's tailoring company established a shop in Dorking at 81-85 High Street, one of a chain of distinctive art deco branches usually built on corner sites, with a billiard hall upstairs. The opening of a new shop was always marked by the unveiling of black marble foundation stones recording family members who attended the ceremony; in Dorking these are clearly visible in Church Passage, flanking the billiard hall's entrance. In December 1940, the *Dorking Advertiser* reported that 'terms suggested by Messrs. Montague Burton Ltd., having been accepted, the air-conditioning plant at their High Street premises is to be adapted to serve the public air raid shelter below those premises'. Burton's

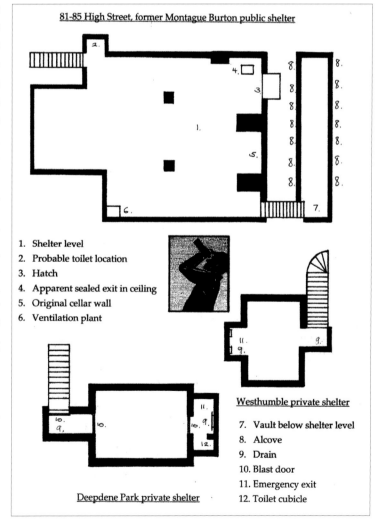

81-85 High Street, former Montague Burton public shelter

1. Shelter level
2. Probable toilet location
3. Hatch
4. Apparent sealed exit in ceiling
5. Original cellar wall
6. Ventilation plant

Deepdene Park private shelter

Westhumble private shelter

7. Vault below shelter level
8. Alcove
9. Drain
10. Blast door
11. Emergency exit
12. Toilet cubicle

Above: A rare piece of surviving Dorking deco: the former Montague Burton's. Above right: One of two foundation stones from the store's 1938 opening.

Below left: Montague Burton's Dorking shelter. Part of the far wall is from an earlier cellar. A delivery hatch in the centre was closed and reinforced for wartime use.
Below right: The shelter below Boots Opticians, still with the original electrics on the columns. Compare the concrete ceiling with the one at 294 High Street.

made another appearance in the press later, along with Quick's, asking if they could add electric sockets below so that shelterers arriving cold and tired could at least warm themselves with a cup of tea.

Somehow, the shelter has survived, and it's fascinating. It is entered from Boots Opticians and stretches the width and depth of the whole building, including the adjacent British Bookshop. Burton's predilection for corner sites meant there was a convenient public entrance in Church Passage and it looks very much like the company ensured that the shelter was fitted out in part at least at its own expense. If you wanted a really secure public refuge, this was the one to choose. From a first look at the descending stairs, with their closely fitting and smooth concrete work, everything signals quality and protection: strengthened ceilings, reinforced by girders, and electric fittings. There is a sense of planning, with no corners being cut or savings made. Even the air conditioner mentioned in the newspaper survives, its handle locked in the open position, its dust filter intact, a piece of British engineering that looks like it would still start at the press of a button.

It is a remarkable jewel of town history. The only thing that could make the shelter better would be if it had retained its wartime signage. Then, flashing a torch around, you find it has. A painted sign states: 'NOTICE. IN THE PUBLIC INTEREST PLEASE PREVENT MIS-USE OF THIS SHELTER AND THE APPARATUS PROVIDED'.

Nearby, there are three attempts at graffiti: BUR (for Burton's), a girl's head and the eyes, nose and whiskers of a cartoon animal. All are unfinished, perhaps interrupted by the arrival of a Burton's manager or a shelter marshal. The only wistful note is the thought that if this is how a shelter for 120 people looks, what was the one for 420 in Farnborough Passage like?

As if this basement doesn't contain enough history, a section of one wall reveals more. It is built from stone, clearly part of an earlier cellar that was vastly expanded when Burton's was built in 1938. Before then, the land had been occupied by very old

Top left: Wartime notice to shelterers. Top middle and top right: Unfinished graffiti.
Middle right: Original shelter internal door, with next to it the green-painted housing for the ventilating machinery. Below right: From the 'Dorking Advertiser', December 1940: 'The air-conditioning plant … is to be adapted to serve the public air raid shelter below (Burton's).'

houses that neighboured St Martin's and Church Passage. Only in the 19th century were those residences given over to trade, housing, as William Dinnage recorded, 'Mr.W.Cole, the leather cutter, and his daughter' and, next door, 'the old-established land and estate agents, Messrs. Alexander and Archibald White'. One of those old, probably 18th century or earlier houses had another of those Dorking double deck cellars: a working basement with, beneath it, a second sand-carved one. In 1938, it was clearly of no use to the modern Burton's shop. Yet a decision must have been taken to preserve it; experience shows that would be unlikely today.

Below the shelter, down a further flight of stairs, is a narrow, fairly low arched passage mined from the sandstone. The best guess is that this is the deep level cellar, probably used to store the beer, wines and perhaps comestibles of a quite grand house above. Its stone was smoothed to remove the pick marks of its creation, and 14 fine,

Below: Below the shelter, carved from the sandstone, and floored and alcoved in brick, a much earlier cellar is preserved. Below right: Reverse view. Bottom right: Wartime survivor: a child's toy pram.

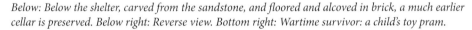

Above: 8 West Street.
Above middle: Cellar turned shelter. The shelves are neatly labelled from the building's time as a pet shop.
Above right: Stairs down, with curved ceiling.

pointed-arched alcoves built into its sides. In the days of the shelter, it was clearly out of bounds but provided a resting place for materials and, perhaps, for its lost property office: a child's toy pram, jam and meat paste jars, a tin for paraffin, a lid for a saucepan and another for that most important weapon of the home front, a kettle.

When it came to shelter, many people took matters into their own hands. No.8 West Street is a fine-beamed old building, probably originally a residence, and now home to Malthouse Antiques. An old stairway, beneath an original, nicely curving ceiling, leads into a cellar that is cement-lined throughout except for one small room, which has the original brick walls. It also has one section where the earlier, higher ceiling and laths are visible. In contrast, the rest of the cellar is lower thanks to a girder and concrete ceiling immediately recognisable as the strengthening necessary to turn it into an effective bomb shelter. What would have been a coal hatch down from the pavement was also rendered at the same time, making it suitable as an emergency exit. Two ventilation pipes were added to the ceiling. Like similar private shelters under the Cricketers and Old House at Home pubs and Scotts the Jewellers, this must have been expensively converted to provide a high standard of protection, and even some comfort, to the occupiers of the building.

When the bombs came, it would be no good complaining that the nearest public shelter was too far away, too crowded and too flimsy. Most people made their own preparations; some had government help, using the excellent Anderson and Morrison shelters, which were supplied at cost price or free to those on low incomes. Others by commissioning built or prefabricated shelters. Most of these were constructed by local builders, often to a noticeably high standard; this is the reason a number still survive, often concealed within or beneath a rockery.

A good example (which has been a stalwart of the Heritage Open Days, on show alongside the owners' award-winning collection of historic stationary engines)

Right: The entrance to Westcott's best-known underground air raid shelter.
Far right: Inside the shelter. Leaning in the corner is a carrier for German incendiary bombs.

remains in Westcott. If Dorking's surface shelters were disliked, then Westcott's were hated. Cold, small, prone to flooding, they were a particular affront to the village's population, which had made clear that they wanted refuges dug into its soft-rock slopes.

A private shelter was sunk into a front garden in Chapel Lane by the then householder, builder Ron Johnson. It was made to the highest standards, with a stepped entrance down, electric lighting and even a little vestibule. It must have been fantastically secure. Even after it was finished, whenever he had any concrete left over from another job he would wheelbarrow it home and add it to the top of the ever-growing shelter mound, which is now an attractive rockery.

Another excellent example of how good privately built shelters sometimes were lies at Pilgrim's Way, Westhumble. No rockery could conceal this one though: its footprint is more of a giant's bootprint, a landscaped slope that conceals a structure so well appointed that it could be mistaken for an official bunker. Almost everything required is here: ventilation, a handrail, drains, an unusual emergency exit reached by climbing a sloping wall upwards, and a mass of protective concrete. So much so that the main shelter room is surprisingly small and, with its arched ceiling, crypt-like. (Shelters usually were; they weren't the blast-doored bunkers of the nuclear age, with room for two weeks' worth of supplies, but were typically designed to hold a family of four for, at the very most, one night.)

It's deep too, seventeen stairs worth. The staircase is separate, to deflect blast from the main room, which was guarded, as they usually were, by a simple wooden door. The only curious omission is electricity, even though the fumes from a paraffin lantern hung from the hook installed for that purpose quickly become noticeable. All in all it's a particularly nice, unchanged and maybe unchangeable survivor in whose metaphorical hands the inhabitants could and did place their lives.

Above left: The shelter was particularly well fitted.
Above middle: Paraffin shelter heater and emergency lighting.
Above: Despite the refuge being well buried the protective mound above it just kept growing and growing – and is now a rockery.

Below left: The beast within: the shelter is inside this slope. The emergency exit is below the potted tree, the entrance is to the right by the wooden hatch.
Below: Keeping the staircase separate supplies the shelter with an internal blast wall.

Another fine example of how durable, if costly, domestic shelters could be survives on the Deepdene Park Estate. The owners of the house in whose garden it was sunk must have been both farsighted and decisive (and perhaps terrified of the kind of vast poison gas bombing raid shown in HG Wells' influential 1936 film *Things To Come*). When they sold their home in September 1939, as the Second World War started, they offered with it a newly desirable feature, described as 'a strong dug-out with lavatory, air filtration plant and emergency exit'. It had cost £268 6s 2d, which was a small fortune: enough to buy a small flat and a third of the cost of the Dorking High Street shelter for 420 people. Its owners got their money's worth. This was the Ritz of bomb shelters. Even today it remains impressive, more bunker than Anderson, with levels of protection usually associated with the nuclear age: an entrance lobby, electric lighting and heavily-locking metal doors, with tiny grille-protected glass peepholes set in them. Even the (chemical) toilet cubicle had its own lightswitch. Notably, and unusually for a private shelter, it could be made gasproof. Above each door is an airhole, each of which can be closed off. Ventilation would then be via a large pipe, which may once have held a hand pump and gas filter.

Pippbrook (the 'House' was only added when the new town hall opened in 1984) may have been the centre of unpopular decisions on shelters but it was also the heart of civil defence in Dorking. It was here that the ARP had its improvised bunker headquarters and where the moving of 3,000 London evacuees from Dorking Halls to their allocated accommodation was arranged. A large first aid post was built below, while the town's air raid siren sat on the roof. From here too was organised the all-important work of the rescue and firewatching parties and the WVS (Women's Voluntary Service),

who supplied food, tea, clothes and comfort to the evacuated, the bombed and the emergency services. Up top was parked the motley collection of donated and adapted vehicles (a loaned Rolls Royce, a Buick, an old Morris, a reworked Armstrong Siddeley saloon) that made up the ARP ambulance and WVS mobile canteen fleet.

With some glitches (embarrassingly, in 1940 the ARP Controller was summonsed after a bright light was seen showing in his office, attracting a crowd who were 'adopting a rather hostile attitude', and fined £20.), the work continued until VE day. Appropriately it was at Pippbrook that, an hour after the end of hostilities in Europe, 'the heads of the Civil Defence Service in the Dorking Urban District received the official thanks of the town for their faithful work throughout the war'.

The current Pippbrook House is the third on the site. The earliest dated back to the 14th century, built on land owned by Walter and Alicia atte Pyppe. It lasted until 1758, then was pulled down and a new mansion constructed. Although its medieval predecessor left little trace, the new great house is shown in a painting (c.1770) of an early cricket match being played on Cotmandene. Some of the structure of that house remains, especially down below, retained in the structure of its replacement, which was commissioned by William Henry Forman, a hugely wealthy ironmaster and mine owner. His chosen architect was the great gothic revivalist Sir George Gilbert Scott. The resulting 1858 exterior was not Scott's best work but the interiors were and are superb, a confection of monographed panelling and painted ceilings that went on to make it such a pleasure to visit when the building was in use as Dorking's library.

Above left: Inside the surprisingly modern and nuclear era-looking, but 1939-built shelter. The hatch leads to the emergency exit and adjoining toilet cubicle. The ventilation pipe on the right may have originally had a hand pump attached.
Above, top to bottom: Mains electricity was provided; did the owner have a terror of gas? The shelter could be completely sealed; and both entry doors have armoured peepholes and multiple closures and bolts

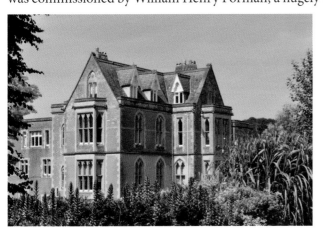

Far left: Pippbrook House.

Above: Pippbrook is attractive outside and superbly decorated within.

The sales particulars from 1890 indicate the then size of the estate of this 'commodious well arranged family mansion'. As well as the house and 'delightful pleasure grounds and gardens tastefully laid out', there was an entrance lodge, stables, a farm, smithy, eleven cottages, an orchard, paddocks and a meadow.

In 1931, Pippbrook became Dorking's town hall and the billiard room became the council chamber. It remained in service until the 1984 opening of the new town hall when, in an imaginative move, the house was rented by Mole Valley District Council (MVDC) to Surrey County Council (SCC) for use as the town library, opening its rather lovely interior up to the public as never before. In 2011, despite pleas and protests, SCC relocated the library, leaving Pippbrook unoccupied. It is strongly hoped that a way can be found to retain this popular public property in public use.

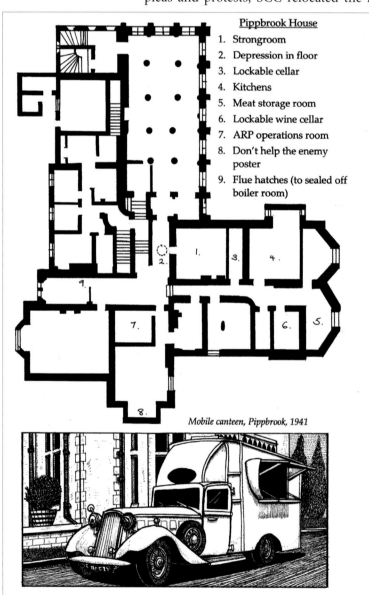

Pippbrook House

1. Strongroom
2. Depression in floor
3. Lockable cellar
4. Kitchens
5. Meat storage room
6. Lockable wine cellar
7. ARP operations room
8. Don't help the enemy poster
9. Flue hatches (to sealed off boiler room)

Mobile canteen, Pippbrook, 1941

The cellars at Pippbrook reflect its time as the town hall and continue to serve as document storage for MVDC. The house's earlier history can be traced there too. The basements contain a sealed hatch here, a bricked-off doorway there, an interior wall so big it must have once been the front of the house, a possible one-time carriage entrance lost among later enclosures. Although the sinks and ranges have all been removed there are reminders of life below stairs in the ironmaster's house: a former meat room with wickedly sharp hooks hanging from its ceiling, a tiled former kitchen area with big slate shelves for food preparation, a lockable wine cellar containing brick bins with incised numbers, and another room, possibly a gun or document room, that is similarly equipped with a heavy door with ventilation holes and a fitted bar that can be padlocked across it. Next door is a large, concrete-roofed, barred strongroom guarded by a combination-locked safe door, that must have once held the council's coffers. In the corridor just outside the vault a round depression in the floor may mark the site of the old mansion's original well.

A mezzanine floor sits on top of the original, now bricked-off boiler room and may cover more of the earlier cellar or even the cellars of the older mansion. However, the most evocative room has to be the one described in the *Dorking Advertiser* five months before the war began: 'The Dorking Report Centre at Pippbrook is now excellently equipped to act as headquarters for A.R.P. work. It consists of rooms in the semi-basement with walls and ceilings strengthened to make them as bombproof as possible. There are telephones for incoming and outgoing messages. The messages are passed from the telephone room to the control room via a pigeon-hole in a door. In the room to which the messages go, there are the officials in control of the various essential A.R.P. services and by them, orders are issued for the dispatch of the required squads. A big framed board hangs on a wall and upon it, by means of discs, the officials can show the number of the various squads on duty, the positions to which the squads have been sent, and other information.' Thanks to that description it is still possible to locate the former ARP operations room, now given over to mobile shelving, and recapture some of the intensity of human effort that went on down below during the war years, as alarms and false alarms were sounded, as bombs and later flying bombs fell.

Above, top to bottom: The safe door entrance to the large former vault; secure room; and history's odds and ends live on underground.
Top left: Secure room.
Top middle: The wine cellar.
Above left: Just one part of the Pippbrook cellars.
Above middle: Tiled and slate-shelved former kitchen.

Far left: The opening in the door identifies the former ARP report centre
Left: Through the hatch, the old ARP operations room, now used for document storage.

During World War Two, every school had to have at least one air raid shelter. Powell Corderoy School's are now buried under Wickes in the old quarries of Vincent Lane, where composer Vaughan Williams filled sandbags in between visits to Dorking Halls, built to stage his music festival and itself sited in yet another former sand quarry. (Dorking Museum has a nice handwritten note from him to his fellow firewatchers Headed 'Issue of Fire Helmets': it requests, 'Please at your convenience send me your head measurements unless you already have a helmet.')

John Molyneux, born in 1937, was a Powell Corderoy pupil. One of his earliest memories is of what happened when the air raid siren sounded: 'We lined up in twos and marched off. The things I most remember about the shelters were the slatted benches and the stale, damp smell.'

Sondes Place School's shelter was lost to later landscaping. Inquiries at other schools have not turned up anything. It was in the nature of school shelters, whether surface or underground, that they were rarely usable for any other purpose. Since

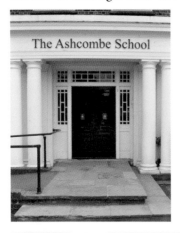

Top: *Inside the shelter.*
Middle left: Looking up
the emergency exit. The
ladder has long since been
removed. On the left is a
large pipe for ventilation.
Middle right: The pipe
is wide enough to have
allowed objects such as
tennis balls, a football and
single shoes to have made
their way in – by accident
or design.
Bottom: Ventilation pipe.

Above: Condensation.
Above right: The emergency exit at the other end of the shelter.

the 1960s, they have been covered or knocked down, buried under new gyms, playgrounds and car parks. More or less every month, around Britain one is unexpectedly found during construction on a school site, its existence having been forgotten. Sometimes, a week is found to give the pupils a look before demolition. Despite their great strength, the shelters have been a transitory phenomenon, changing within a decade from a vital necessity to an inefficient use of space. A temporary aberration in history, to be removed or smoothed away.

So, the surviving structure at the Ashcombe School is not just a lucky survivor, it is probably the only one of its type in the whole town. This makes it particularly fortunate that the school was kind enough to break it open to allow it to be recorded and photographed for this book.

It's a slit trench type (the most common for schools): a narrow, concrete-roofed corridor, buried under a mound of earth. Nothing revolutionary, except that you're reminded that when Surrey County Council did build shelters, they built them well. Normally, one like this has an entrance and an emergency exit, often where the screened chemical toilet was positioned for reasons of ventilation. This one has two emergency ways out. It is concrete throughout, with gutters running from the toilet area (presumably in case of spillage) to the well-sunken entry door. At one end there is a large gauge ventilation pipe but smaller, now-filled airholes appear regularly, alternating high and low, so that warmer, breathed air would rise and exit, while fresh air would come in through the lower apertures. In case of gas attack everyone would don their gasmasks. Children would have sat on narrow benches running the shelter's length, which have now gone. There is evidence that there was an electricity supply for lighting and, among the detritus, a small electric filament heater survives.

Right: The shelter would be a treasure trove for a collector of scientific glassware of the late 20th century.

Above: More scientific glassware.
Left: Small electric heater.
Below left: Possible remains of duckboarding.
Below right: The shelter is woodlice heaven; spiders, slugs and snails are also well represented.

Subterranea Britannica is the society for British underground archaeology. One of its members, Mark Rogers, was a pupil in the 1970s. He recalled: 'They used to store chemical supplies, and there was a case of the Fire Brigade being called to smoke emerging when something unstable started to fume.' The scorch marks from that incident are still visible and the shelter is filled with a museum's worth of late 20th century science lab glassware: retorts, flasks and pipettes still stored in wooden boxes that crumble away when touched. It's as it should be in times of peace. Where children once sat clutching their gasmasks, at first perhaps in terror, and later with boredom and discomfort, a variety of spiders, earwigs, snails and slugs now lay claim to the damp and darkened spaces.

CHAPTER FIVE
Trade secrets

In order to survive, a town must offer a balanced range of services and goods to its inhabitants and those of its hinterland. Shops come and go, as the fashions for the goods they offer ebb and flow, in a carousel of openings and closures; several toy shops, then none; multiple chemists; dairies and grocers giving way to supermarkets; sudden flowerings of bookshops or sellers of radio sets and electrical goods, gun shops, milk bars and bicycle stores. Dorking's status as a market town led to the presence not just of butchers, bakers and candlemakers but also solicitors, auction houses, land agents, agricultural suppliers, feed merchants, piano salesmen, outfitters, bonnet makers and more. Industries such as stone and lime quarrying, brickmaking, ironwork, coachmaking and vehicle manufacture have come and, largely, gone. Many have left behind secret spaces.

It would be wrong to assume that to be interesting a cave must belong to a castle, a historic inn or be a rich man's caprice. Below the town's houses, shops and workplaces squat a multitude of hidden spaces, sometimes used, more often lost, little remembered and atmospherically derelict. It was so easy to have a hand carved cellar in Dorking. Why would anyone resist? The following are just a few examples.

West Street has the most surviving ancient buildings of all the town's compass-pointed thoroughfares. A walk along it reveals a multitude of grilles, hatches and windows at pavement level. The West Street frontage of 2 South Street is typical. A blocked doorway, barred cellar window and air vent, plus a low door that opens onto the cellar stairs, all indicate that it has a basement running the length of the building. This, along with Nos. 4 and 6, make up what in 1649 was known as the House by the Well, a large detached residence that, much altered, enlarged and then refronted in the early 19th century, has occupied this dominant position in the town for at least four centuries. Number 2, which straddles both the High and West Streets, has housed many different establishments: a bakery; R Fielder, Victorian-era draper, clothier and shoe manufacturer, a milliners and a photographic shop. It is now home to Bakehouse.

Below left: Pump Corner and The Old House at the Well.
Below right: The cellars at 2 South Street have been adapted for use as an office and stock room.

Above: 19 West Street, built as Dorking's Temperance Hotel.

In recent years, the large cellar has been completely lined and floored to allow it to be used as an office and stock room. It has been suggested in print that an early second bakery cellar, complete with ovens, was blocked off in the 19th century and still remains, dark and walled in, under the busy roadway. There is no evidence of this.

The neighbouring premises at No.4 South Street have overlooked Pump Corner, the heart of the early town, for the same length of time. Now Dorking Stoves, it was long the home first of TG Rix's café and then the luncheon and tea rooms of Loyns, the 'Electric Machine Bakers', advertised as dating back to 1749. There is no known cellar here, which is surprising given its use, situation and long history. Possibly the fact that its front wall literally touches the old town well (probably as a result of the addition of the 19th century façade) gave rise to fears that any cellar would suffer from dampness. There is, however, a rumour of some form of small but covered void below.

Dorking was a town sodden with inns, pubs and beerhouses. So it's no surprise that it attracted the notice of the Victorian temperance movement, in the form of the larger than life Elizabeth Cotton, Lady Hope. She was an Australian evangelical Christian teetotaller, prodigious tract writer, preacher, Sunday school teacher and founder of a coffee room, complete with bible classes and prayer meetings, that was designed to preserve the town's working class from the temptations of alcohol. By her own account, she was a gifted advocate for total abstinence, whose words would almost instantly bring to Jesus a profuse collection of slumdwellers, railwaymen, limekiln workers, miners, 'gypsies, thieves, thugs' and Dorking's 'wild boys who thronged the streets on Sunday afternoons, uncared for and untaught'. A possible alternative view might be that she was a self-publicising busybody.

In 1877 she had married a rich retired admiral 34 years her senior. On his death four years later she inherited his fortune and title. Later she wed another wealthy and much older businessman and philanthropist. When he died she contested his will, which provided for her but, in her opinion, left too much of his estate to his children. To mount the challenge she unwittingly employed a conman who then took all her money.

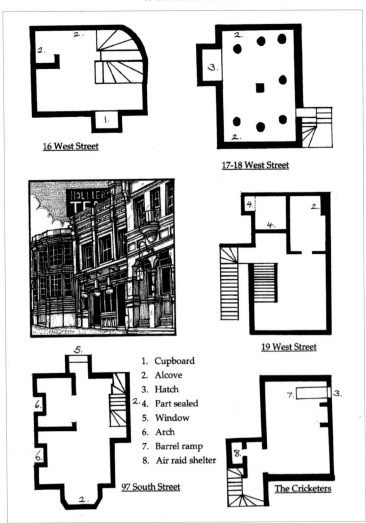

16 West Street

17-18 West Street

19 West Street

1. Cupboard
2. Alcove
3. Hatch
4. Part sealed
5. Window
6. Arch
7. Barrel ramp
8. Air raid shelter

97 South Street

The Cricketers

Lady Hope died aged 79 in her native Australia, leaving behind a monument to her beliefs in the shape of the former Temperance Hotel, now Harmans Bespoke Furniture, at 19 West Street.

This building embodied the ideals of the Temperance movement and did so with considerable style. The well-preserved frontage and ground floor lobby have lost none of their power to impress. Inevitably, since this is Dorking, it was built opposite one pub and a minute's stroll from four more.

The hotel's cellar has two entrances: one from the lobby, which was visible to guests and graced by an attractive wooden staircase, and a much more utilitarian brick and cement one at the rear. The space below is neat, square and functional. This is the late 19th century in action: the shadowed, atmospheric carved caverns of the earlier hostelries have been replaced with a more scientific use of space. The cellar is smaller than those of the competing inns; presumably, the hotel's stock in trade of cordials and soft drinks did not require the space demanded by barrels of beer, cider, old tom, rum, brandy and whisky.

Number 19 is one in a row of three imposing old buildings. Its neighbour, Nos.17-18 (Dorking House Antiques), reveals that it has a cellar below by its airbricks and a double hatch in the pavement. For much of the 19th century, this was the home of Hollier's Teas. William Dinnage remembered it well: 'The next most notable establishment was that of the tea-taster and tea specialist, Mr. William Hollier. This gentleman occupied the premises for many years, as did his father before him. (He) delivered tea for many miles around Dorking, both in Surrey and Sussex, and Hollier's tea

was a very well-known commodity.' The company was the major advertiser on the horsedrawn 1897 Dorking omnibus, which still makes appearances around the town during Heritage Open Days. Behind – and below – the façade, the building appears even older than its elegant neo-classical frontage suggests. Unusually, the cellar, with its closed-off delivery trapdoors and twin candle

Top: The staircase down from the hotel foyer is attractively made in wood.
Above: The cellar is now subdivided into three rooms.

Left above: 17-18 West Street, Dorking House Antiques.
Far left: All but one of the supporting columns are treetrunks.
Left: Reverse view, with candle/lamp alcove to right and an unused safe to the left.

Right: 16 West Street, the New Fountain Garden. Far right: The cellar at number 16, complete with candle alcove.

alcoves, is supported not by the usual beams or brick columns, but almost entirely by actual treetrunks.

The third building in the row is No.16 (The New Fountain Garden restaurant), housed in a particularly fine double bayed and weatherboarded 18th century building with a 16th century wing at the rear, behind which a forgotten and covered-over well was discovered (you can see the pond set atop it from the stairs leading to the Waitrose car park). The cellar, entered via a trapdoor in the floor of the restaurant, is modest and neat. It's also surprisingly small, given the house's later 19th century commercial history as Bolland's greengrocer and confectioner. Perhaps there might once have been another space below or behind the oldest part of the building that, like the well, was sealed and forgotten.

Back on South Street, the gardens of Rose Hill House were once accessed via its gothic arch. Since the 1860s, it has led instead to the newly-created Rose Hill Estate, the town's first garden suburb. Among the large Victorian houses created around a rising central meadow, on which sheep still graze, is No.11 Rose Hill. This has a short arched tunnel driven into the bank on which it sits. Visited in 1968, it was described then as being blocked at one end (where it may have originally entered the cellars of the house above) and having a second bore running alongside it, partitioned into six foot arched lengths. Reportedly used in recent decades for storing telephone poles,

Below: 11 Rose Hill, with bricked-off cellar tunnel entrance to left of the arch. Below right: Photographed using a fibre optic probe: the short tunnel, with tree roots in foreground, arches to storage bins on left.

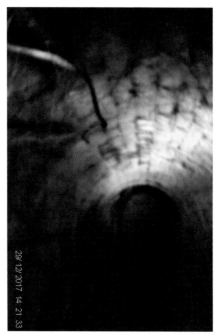

the single entrance, which is visible from the street, has now been bricked over. The whole construction appears to have been a storage tunnel for the house, built to hold fuel, perishables and wine.

Just around the corner, 97 South Street is a handsome early 19th century house, constructed by a local builder as his home and office (across the road a frieze atop the elegant gothic frontage proclaims 'Bartholemews Press & Builders &c. Offices Opposite'). This was the home of someone who had arrived. A gentleman's house, in the leafy lane of South Street, away from the bustle of the town centre. And with the details to match. A fine iron arched iron entrance porch (when a doctor had a house built across the road he is said to have asked for one in the same style), window bays, pilasters, cornices, twin entrance stairways and a cellar, with room for coal, of course, but drinks too. In 1910, the house became a dental practice and it has stayed as one since (now run by Dr Michael Fleming). Down below, along with the Christmas decorations and workaday cleaning materials, are reminders of over a century of dentistry; a compendium of items neatly put away ready for a use that did not always arrive before a newer and better version appeared, leaving behind a pleasing mix of neatly packed and stored textbooks (Dental Radiography, 1916), medicine bottles, tools, kidney dishes, Neutralin Tablets, Skin Stain Remover (for Silver Stains), Impression compound, Pulp Caps and X-Ray Film (Open in Dark Room Only) .

It's rare that a site is far more intriguing than its initial description (often it's the other way round, with what are described as mysterious tunnels running under the town's roads turning out to be coal cellars). On one of the South Street cave tours a visitor mentioned a sand cellar beneath the long-established Dorking Tool Hire shop at Mount House, 98-100 South Street. Anyone who was a customer there or at the

Top left: 97 South Street, home to a dental and other practices.
Top right: The cellar at 97 South Street.
Middle left: Reverse view.
Middle right: An arch built for bottles is still holding some.
Bottom left and bottom middle: The cellar preserves reminders of over a century of dentistry.

Above top: Mount House in the process of renovation.
Above: Mount House is a treasure trove of surviving historic features.

Right: The stairs down from the kitchen lead first to the top cellar then to a further level below.
Far right: The nicely beamed upper cellar, with arch on left and cavity next to the stairs. The brick floor is pitched to deliver water to a drain below this.

1970s and 80s army surplus shop that preceded it (RAF greatcoats £6, gasmasks £5) is likely to have noticed the huge historic fireplace and fine old staircase, reminders of the building's history as a 17th century private house.

Following the tool hire company's relocation to Betchworth, renovation began on the building in 2018. The modernisation is intended to preserve and incorporate the many superb surviving historical features of the building but the installation of shuttering around the site signalled that there wouldn't be another chance for some time to visit the reported cellar. A request for access was met with the reply 'Let me give you a tour'.

What lies below is one of the most pleasantly puzzling of all the underground sites in Dorking. Down six steps (wide and solid enough to show that they were intended for frequent use, probably while carrying loads), there is a cellar that offers various possibilities as to its purpose. In the 19th century, this part of South Street was a mix of farms, builders, masons, private houses (some very substantial), cottages, a slaughterhouse, tithe barn, market gardens and meadows. So what was this basement meant to hold? It has a large arch that could store practically anything, from firewood to sacks of grain, drink to cheeses. It has multiple alcoves but they're too shallow for bottles or barrels and too numerous to be candle alcoves, though very suitable for jars of preserves and dried goods. In one wall a deep square, brick-lined cavity runs for around eight feet (2.4 metres) before a more modern wall terminates it. It could be an oven but there is no aperture below it for fuel, unless it is the early type, seen in stone in some castles, where the fire was raked out before the bread was put in. There is no trough or any feeders for animals, no hooks for meat. Yet the floor is sloped to a drain so that it can be washed down, suggesting this was a working area. There are a number of possibilities: a cider cellar, scullery, dairy or bakery (but one of the fireplaces a floor above includes a bread oven or bacon smoker), a sinkless laundry room, a meat store (but then why the alcoves?). The best bet is that it is a combination: a larder, work area and fuel store that doubled as one of the above but with an unexplained cavity built into one wall.

In the South Street Caves in recent years the lowest room has sometimes been

given the rather melodramatic misnomer of 'the mystery chamber'. What lies beneath this cellar would actually live up to that description.

A second flight of stairs leads down into a roughly circular, almost shaftlike space, off which is a further cave; it is dark, alcoved and teasingly mysterious.

This first space is two storeys below the ground. Yet it has a pit in the middle, lined with a jagged curve of old masonry, that sinks further still, while above there is no roof until it hits the bottom of the shop floor above.

It's a fascinating place, which demands that you use detective skills to address the puzzles of history. Is the curved wall the remains of a well, icehouse or water tank, or maybe a buried kiln? Could this house have knowingly been built over one, or is it more likely that the continuation of the shaft right up to the ground floor joists reveals a long distant collapse? If so the spoil has been removed and the damage made good; the walls are pickmarked and rounded and there's remedial cement work at the top. The pit is too shallow to be a well, unless it was competently filled. Very competently; its floor feels entirely firm and, for no evident reason, has the beginnings of a short arched tunnel dug off to one side. It is not unreminiscent of the wellshaft in *The Silence of the Lambs*.

The puzzle continues. Next to this chamber is a rather good example of a Dorking cave dating back at least to the 18th century. Here the alcoves are deep enough to store bottles. Tally marks, like the ones in the South Street Caves, have been marked in the soft sandstone wall. A large raised bench at the end could have held several barrels, enough for a large household or a workforce employed in a field surrounding it.

If it can be fairly confidently asserted that this is a genuinely atmospheric and

Far left: Stairs down and alcoves, with brick joists supporting the curved wall above.
Above left: The cellar is part illuminated by one window, which originally had a staircase outside largely covering it.
Above: While another, older, barred window has long ago been bricked over.

Above left: Below the cellar is an almost three storey cavern stretching up to the underneath of the ground floor...
Above: ...down to the floor level of the cave...
Far left: ...and then down to a pit with the beginnings of a side tunnel dug in it.
Left: The view from the pit.

Above, left to right: The cave cellar. Set in its middle is a later, badly-built wall that almost blocks it.
The reverse view. Through the doorway is the shaftlike chamber.
The metal cabinet set in the wall.

antique storage cellar, then the question remains: why did whoever later faced some alcoves with bricks also divide it in half with a crudely made wall apparently designed only to contain an enigmatic metal cabinet? This appears to be a small bread oven, especially as it is decorated in a rather French rustic style with antique tools for cutting and threshing wheat. But there is no flue and no way to heat it. It isn't a strongbox because it lacks a lock. The brickwork also appears too modern for it to have held the instruments to conduct a clandestine religious service.

There may be a pleasing possibility that it is a former oven repurposed to hold something for use below rather than above. Is it too fanciful to wonder if it contained snuff, tobacco or drinking glasses? Perhaps installing it was an apprentice's task but the question remains: why it was set in an ugly wall rather than a convenient alcove? Could the cellar have been used for drinking parties or tastings of its stock, perhaps while sitting on that barrel bench, even if in later years it meant squeezing through the little passage that had to be dug out to get round the wall? That possibility arises because not all of the carved names, some with punctuation, roman numerals and grand flourishes, look like those of Dorking servants: Casimiy Daniel 1795; J.B; Downey V, R, I Overlong, "M"; E.S; Curran; John Swayne Born In (or Born Jan) 1764;

Above left: Beyond the wall.
Above right: The sandstone of the alcoves is flecked with ironstone.
Right: You find everything underground. Even the kitchen sink.

Old wine; 1767; 1760; 1798; JP 1917; (an illegible sentence ending) …1796 adiele; RAIS; R BROOK XMAS 1901; CWB; GOOSE; Borinie; Grape or Crape.

Archive research by Sue Tombs of Dorking Museum has filled a number of gaps in what is known about Mount House, which was referred to in John Attlee's *Reminiscences of Old Dorking* as being home to 'Mr Richard Clapton, an independent old gentleman'. He was born in 1767 and died in Dorking in 1848, aged 81. According to the land tax records and the 1840 tithe map, he was the occupier but the house was owned by Heathfield Young, brewer, landlord and owner of local pubs and inns.

The John Swayne who incised his name with great decorative sweeping lines, was baptised at St Martin's church in 1764. His father, also named John, was a surgeon and parish apothecary. They both lived in Dorking, possibly in Mount House. On his death in 1773, the father left 'all the Drugs, Medicines and utensells in my Shop together with all my Instruments and Books of Physic and Surgery' to his son John, the cellar name carver, who is therefore likely to have also been a surgeon. His brother William inherited the lease of a farm at Merrow, where the family name lives on as Swayne's Lane.

This positive identification from the graffiti is particularly interesting, and a rare example of a guest or homeowner, rather than a servant or worker, venturing below. People leave their names behind in order to be remembered. In this case it has worked across the centuries. Poignantly, by 1793 John Swayne was dead, aged just 29.

Opposite Mount House lived another character whose history has come down to us: Major Peter Labelliere (1725–1800), still remembered for being buried upside down on Box Hill.

Although he was the son of Huguenot refugees and without any formal education, Labelliere had managed to become both a teacher and an officer of Marines before he settled in Dorking. Despite receiving an annual pension of £100 from the Duke of Devonshire and a standing invitation to spend a month a year at his house, he took lodgings in the upstairs room of a small South Street cottage known as the Hole in the Wall. Below him lived a widowed seamstress and her children (if one was rebellious, Labelliere would exhort him or her to 'Come down, proud Jack'; any noisy fights were greeted by a parade ground voice from upstairs instructing 'Order below!').

As well as being a deeply religious and charitable man, Labelliere was also a political radical, in favour of liberty, freedom of expression and, by implication, independence for the American colonies. He took to walking around the town singing hymns, declaiming on politics and quoting the Bible. His appearance and personal hygiene deteriorated and he became known as 'the walking dunghill'.

Walk he did, every day, in Dorking and on Box Hill, a place he loved, and where he lost an eye in odd circumstances. In 1799 he returned from a visit to the Duke of Devonshire and told his landlady 'Now I have come back to live and die with you, for this day nine months (or tomorrow nine-months) I shall depart out of

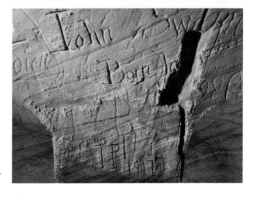

Below: The cave is rich in graffiti, Including the unusually named Casimiy Daniel of 1795, of whom no records can be found. …And an almost too faint to read 1796 inscription that appears to end in 'adiele'. John Swayne signed his name with a great long decorative tail to the 'y' and a sweeping curlicue that encircled the word 'Born'.

Major Peter Labelliere's grave, in the spot that he loved.

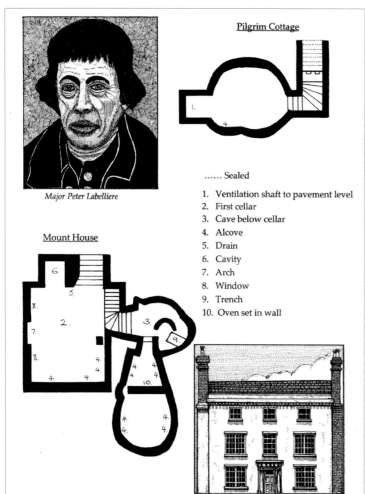

Major Peter Labelliere

Mount House

Pilgrim Cottage

...... Sealed

1. Ventilation shaft to pavement level
2. First cellar
3. Cave below cellar
4. Alcove
5. Drain
6. Cavity
7. Arch
8. Window
9. Trench
10. Oven set in wall

this world.' Which he did, not quite on the prophesied day, after what was described as great suffering. A witness at his deathbed said 'He stretched out his arms, then gently folded them, and died like a lamb'.

The interment of this popular, thoroughly good but deeply troubled man was conducted in accordance with his wishes, on unconsecrated ground, without religious rites, and with joy. It was more like a holiday or fair day than a funeral, attracting 'a vast concourse of the inhabitants of Dorking', plus day trippers down from the capital caught up in the spectacle. The coach carrying the coffin was preceded by two carts distributing branches of yew and box, the two trees Labelliere had most admired on the hill. The thousands of people present carried or waved them as they climbed the slope, to where workmen had dug a 10 foot deep hole described as being just like a wellshaft. Many dropped their branches into the hole to cushion what was going to be placed there: Labelliere's coffin. He had paid two of the landlady's children to dance on it. The boy happily did. His older sister Elizabeth, aged nine, didn't think it was quite right to do so. She sat on it instead.

Head down, feet upwards, the casket was inserted into the hole. More branches were added and it was then filled. It remains today, which the bridge over the Mole no longer did. While the celebratory burial had been taking place, more of the town's naughty boys had destroyed the wooden footbridge back. The mourners all had to take a lengthy detour or ford the river.

The explanation for the unorthodox burial seems to be that Labelliere believed that on judgement day the world would be turned upside down. His head down position would allow him to meet God standing face to face. *The Gentleman's Magazine* of July 1800 awarded him a deserved epitaph: 'No political reformer more ardently desired social changes; and none ever used more mild and gentle methods to gain the fulfilment of his wishes.'

The best candidate for the Hole in the Wall, or at least the site of it, is Pilgrim

Above left: 39 South Street, probable successor to the Hole in the Wall.
Above middle: Lifting out a section of staircase and removing carpet and a trapdoor allows access. On the right a modern wall seals off half the old staircase down. On the left is a niche for a candle for those descending to the cellar. Above it is the underside of the stairs to the first floor
Above: Looking up the ventilation shaft to the pavement above.
Far left: The remaining half of the staircase down.
Left: The cellar below number 39.

Cottage at 39 South Street, which is managed by the St Saviours Dispersed scheme (part of Riverside Care and Support) and owned by the Churches of Dorking Housing Association. In Labelliere's time at the end of the 18th century, it would have been a very humble cottage surrounded by the gardens and orchards of grander houses. An unusually large and deep ventilation shaft and grille, in plain view from the pavement at the front of the current house, signals the presence of a room underground, but finding it is less easy. It was visited in the 1970s by CSS, who reported that: 'There is no orthodox cellar to the house, but a concealed trapdoor by the stairs leads to a steep flight of steps and thence to a rock-hewn chamber'. Since then half the staircase has been sacrificed to make space for a small ground floor room, in which the original trapdoor probably remains below the floor. A new hatch is accessed, uniquely, by lifting the carpet and a trapdoor and taking out the entire first step of the staircase to the first floor. A brieze block wall with iron rungs replaces the lost seven or so steps, making it possible to climb down to the remaining stairs. These lead to a small, low, carved storage space below the front parlour. It is part lit by the grilled ventilation shaft and clearly would have been well suited to preserving food and drink. Sadly, no early inhabitant carved his or her name in its sandstone walls, nor even a biblical reference or a seditious slogan.

CHAPTER SIX

High Street, low street

There are myths about Dorking's underground that you meet with again and again. A passage from the White Horse to the church, so-called 'brothel tunnels', 'Roman' murals, an underground river or lake with a lost boat moored on its pitch black shores, a tunnel running the length of the High Street. The one that comes nearest to truth is that last one.

Behind the south side of Dorking High Street is, or was, a dark mirror image of the shops that line it. A low road of cellars, shafts, caves and tunnels lay beneath or behind virtually every building. If the walls of each cellar were pierced, it would once have been possible to travel underground from one end of the road to the other, without very much digging. In places, the cluster of excavations is so profuse that it actually stretches belief. Yet they existed or exist there below, reflecting the sheer age and numbers of shops, houses and pubs that have occupied this main thoroughfare and helped make the town what it is.

Below left: A town landmark, the White Horse Hotel conceals a small labyrinth of tunnels beneath it.

On both sides and for its full length, the road is riddled with subterranean spaces. The north side of the High Street (known as East Street until the 20th century) is no slouch when it comes to cellars but, apart from examples such as the Wheatsheaf and Sun Inns, really extensive excavation tended to be restricted by the fact that many of the properties ended at Back Lane, now Church Street. Those opposite had no such constraint: the south side is, or at least was, so hugely and intensively punctured by its own historic underworld

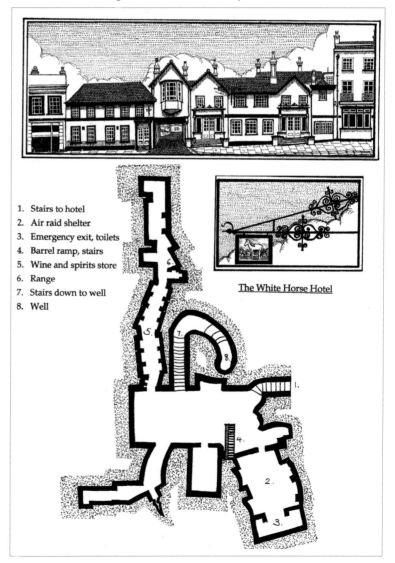

1. Stairs to hotel
2. Air raid shelter
3. Emergency exit, toilets
4. Barrel ramp, stairs
5. Wine and spirits store
6. Range
7. Stairs down to well
8. Well

The White Horse Hotel

Top left: Just the first of the White Horse cellars. The authenticity of the 1671 date is questionable.
Top middle: Barred gate to bayed and alcoved bottle store – and considerably more tunnel space than initially appears.
Top right: From the main cellars a passage continues past the bottle store…
Above: …and into this short, older-looking section…
Above right: …before continuing into a further tunnel, with an antique range looking oddly out of place in it.

that it deserves a chapter to itself.

The White Horse Hotel has been a feature of the High Street since its construction in front of and on top of an older edifice, the 12th century Cross House, named for its ownership (and possibly use as a hostel) by the warrior monks of the Knights Templar and, after their violent suppression, by the Order of St John of Jerusalem. The earlier building featured in two incidents of bloody history, the murder of a chaplain on the premises in 1241 and a 1520 attack by an armed mob on the servant of its then occupant, vicar Miles Hogg.

What is below it is, at first sight, slightly fantastic; far more extensive than expected. When the Cross House was replaced in the 18th century by The White Horse, it incorporated the older structure's foundations and probably some of its masonry. After Deepdene and the South Street Caves, these are Dorking's largest known surviving tunnels. A fairly normal pub cellar, girder and brick roofed, stone and brick flagged, gives off onto unsuspected tunnels and rooms, mostly still in use, many with walls made up of bulging bulwarks of sandstone buttressed by columns of bricks. This is organic growth, reused, modernised, adapted, only sometimes here and there left to decay. There's a very modern barrel room, an original multi-bayed wine and spirits store that stretches much further than you expect into a crudely-niched turn that might even pre-date the building above, and then into another tunnel now used for document storage, with an antique cooking hearth incongruously marooned on a plinth. One large, unused, crumbling, sandstone-walled room reveals the traces of a probable air raid shelter for guests and staff. At its far end, there is a small annexe with a ventilation pipe, emergency exit and a heavily cobwebbed cubicle either side that would fit a chemical toilet.

Just when you think it can't get much better, you remove a panel blocking off a doorway and, instead of revealing another chamber, discover some worn stone steps. The sand floor tilts down, the tunnel turns, there are four more dais-like steps and at its end is the bottom of a dry well.

It's not usual to be able to look up a well rather than down into it. So, which came first, a surface well or an underground one? Was it easier to drive a tunnel into an existing wellshaft in order to draw water by hand, then climb two flights of stairs to the kitchens, instead of cranking it to the surface right by the kitchen door? (If so, it's

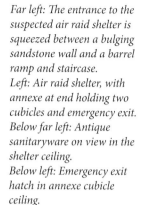

Far left: The entrance to the suspected air raid shelter is squeezed between a bulging sandstone wall and a barrel ramp and staircase.
Left: Air raid shelter, with annexe at end holding two cubicles and emergency exit.
Below far left: Antique sanitaryware on view in the shelter ceiling.
Below left: Emergency exit hatch in annexe cubicle ceiling.

difficult to explain why the passage performs a loop before reaching its objective). Or was the wellshaft dropped onto an existing cellared spring beneath the inn? We don't know and aren't likely to.

The tunnel down to the well shows a tidemark up to the second step, revealing a less disastrous rise and escape of water than in the South Street Caves. A quick fingertip search of the loose sand that fills it immediately turns up fragments of china and 19th century bottles. The entire tunnel is wonderfully marked by its users. Here again are the superb carvings of barely educated potboys, cellarmen and servants who, at a time of widespread illiteracy, nevertheless left us their names in the fine cursive script that would have been thrashed into them in the short period of basic schooling allotted to them. Here are dates: 1761, 1793 (the beginning of the French Revolutionary Wars), 1801, 1811, 1818 (the year of *Frankenstein's* publication), 1819, October 1822. A plethora of remembering, history, names and initials. Etched by hand down here in the near absolute darkness in moments of rest or escape by staff sent to lug water up all those stairs: W Baker, C Clack, Woollett, Jones and Ann Hewett (by 1801 the landlady).

Left to right: Stairs down from the cellar to the well passage.
Looking up the same stairs.
The passage descending to the well.

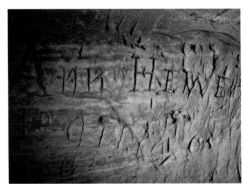

Does her signature show that this was an officially sanctioned place, a social space where the workers could express their individuality, leave a memento, perhaps share tobacco, a joke, a drink or a kiss? Was one of these a serving girl or barman who took Charles Dickens his water and brandy or hot rum and butter, or served him and many others the local delicacies: water sousey (a dish of carp, perch and tench), white snails, a Dorking chicken with its characteristic supernumerary claws? They laboured, lived, perhaps loved here, and little would remain of them if they had not left us their handiwork in these walls.

As the White Horse grew, it incorporated neighbouring properties, including a third of the 16th century Dutch House, one of the town's oldest and prettiest mansions. It had been converted into three houses in 1820. Later the houses became shops and the building's lovely Dutch-gabled frontage was lost to the usual plain Georgian façade, though its fine white-painted 17th century chimneys and roofline can be seen above and behind the hotel's. The house at No.136 inherited a good part of the mansion's cellars, before becoming a chemist from the 19th until the early 21st centuries (Doubleday, then Dixon and later Woodcock.) On market days, a travelling dentist used to set up his chair on the pavement in front and pull teeth, bloodily and without anaesthetic, in front of the crowds. The large metal delivery hatch and lovely etched ruby glass window above the door advertising Idris Table Waters date from those incarnations. In stone and ancient brick, its capacious and atmospherically aged cellars chart those five or more centuries of change, from mansion to pharmacies to barbers. The first basement is approached down a flight of stairs. Off it, a dark, cavelike short passage has been carved into the rock. At its end a recess or aperture down is choked with sand. Down another full flight of stairs lies the cool and heavily alcoved vault that would have held wines, meats, ales and perhaps ice for the great house, and later medicines and their ingredients. Age-encrusted vintage chemist's bottles stand discarded on sand-strewn shelves. One that held gin has been tucked out of sight. A laddered stairway ends at the ceiling, long since sealed off, another climbs to the one-time hatch on the pavement.

The most densely labyrinthine part of the underground high street runs roughly

Top left: Two storeys below the surface, the inn's well, surrounded by the carved names and initials of those who drew water there. An 'I+P' appears both here and the South Street Caves, suggesting that the same person may have worked in – or delivered drink to – both establishments.
Top right: The well was clearly the place where staff were permitted to leave their names and initials.
Above: Looking up the well…
Above right: …and down it. The detritus suggests it fell out of use in the mid 19th century.

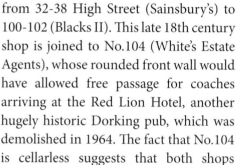

Far left: 94 to 102 High Street, which sit on top of two cellars. Nos.94-98 also used to conceal a substantial tunnel behind the premises. Left: Squeezed between Nos.66 and 70 is the entrance to the one time subterranean wonderland of Farnborough Passage.

from 32-38 High Street (Sainsbury's) to 100-102 (Blacks II). This late 18th century shop is joined to No.104 (White's Estate Agents), whose rounded front wall would have allowed free passage for coaches arriving at the Red Lion Hotel, another hugely historic Dorking pub, which was demolished in 1964. The fact that No.104 is cellarless suggests that both shops were once one house. The cellar at Nos.100-102 is described as being of sandstone now reinforced by concrete. It runs the width of the shop and stops at a brick wall at its front. The wall is rumoured to block a tunnel to the South Street Caves. This is impossible and it is more likely that it is either simply the front wall of the cellar or that it covers a further subcellar scooped out in the recognised Dorking manner by digging under the pavement or even the roadway without permission.

Next door, at 94-98 High Street (Tudor Williams), there are roomy cellars, part lit by pavement lights, with an unused safe still set in place below. However, there is no discernible trace of the historic fifty foot long sandstone tunnel, with a separate shaft to the surface, that could be entered from the rear of the premises as late as the 1980s.

A few doors westwards, between Nos.66 and 70, is Farnborough Passage, which is shown in a particularly attractive 1905 sketch of a 'Quaint old Court Yard, Dorking, Surrey'. It depicts the then grovelike alleyway and court, overshadowed by trees, with rustic stairs framing a doorway dug into the sylvan bank. It's the kind of wonderfully scenic antique niche you'd expect a town to fight to keep. Dorking didn't.

The doorway formed the entrance to a tunnel that stretched behind No.66 (Flowers by Elaine). Dug out for storage, it was also used as a Christmas grotto for many years. It's gone now, buried by modern flats that consumed the ancient courtyard in 2003.

At neighbouring No.62 a tunnel and sand chambers were destroyed for parking in the 1970s, while on the other side, No.70 is now a jewellers (Scotts of Dorking). Like its florist neighbour, it retains a cellar, which is pleasantly eerie, due to its unusually narrow doorways and corridor and the hooks, blood gutter and drains that date back to its long history, until the 1970s, as a butchers. A headbangingly low first room gives onto a lower, subdivided and alcoved working space. An insulated and tiled former coldroom is festooned with hooks and has an aged slate water tank in a corner.

Right: Former meat locker, one of four rooms below number 70.
Far right: The fourth room served as an air raid shelter. Note the reinforced ceiling.
Below: The fourth cellar room. Alcove on left, former trapdoor to pavement on right.
Below right: Tinplate emergency advice notice, showing the long-abandoned Holger Nielsen method of artificial resuscitation.

Handwritten instructions ('Switch down. Fan only. Hand control') and a certificate from the Lightfoot Refrigeration Company remain, along with a tinplate notice on what to do in case of electric shock ('Whilst you are giving artificial respiration instruct someone to cover the patient with a blanket or two and provide hot water bottles … when he has sufficiently recovered make him comfortable and give hot tea.'). In the fourth and largest chamber, a bedstead, strengthened concrete ceiling with filled-in ventilation hole, reinforcing girders and corrugated iron, all suggest use as a domestic bomb shelter.

What of Dorking's largest public air raid shelter (described in Chapter Four), that stretched behind the premises, and was adapted in 1939 from another of the historic cave complexes? Gone, recently consumed by the same flats that doomed the Christmas grotto. Elaine Davis, owner of the flower shop, remembers the subterranean shelter being possible to enter less than twenty years ago. It was dark, brick-lined, still with toilet facilities in place; living history that would have been perfect for visits by schools and the occupants of the town that built it.

Almost unbelievably, picturesque little Farnborough Passage housed a third mysterious old tunnel. Less unbelievably, it appears that this too was razed for the sake of parking and flats.

According to a 1970s visit report by CSS, this subterranean passageway was 140 feet (42.7 metres) long, with an entrance to a further sand cave, and three shafts to the surface, all hidden behind the High Street. It also had yet another entrance three doors down behind No.82. 'There is a derelict garden there now, with a door into another brick-lined chamber in the hillside', they reported. Not any more there isn't.

Next door to Scotts is the Kuoni Shop, at 74 High Street. Until 1913, this was the Rock beerhouse and brewery, run by the Lucock family. It was lyrically recalled by William Dinnage: 'I well recollect, being on occasions in the High-street and passing near the entrance to the Rock brewery, seeing the Lucocks and their men bringing out the open grains in large basket containers and tipping them into farm wagons drawn alongside the high pavement and approached by planks from the pavement to the sides of the wagon. The men wore red caps, and the scent of the grains for me was delicious!'

If it seems surprising that they could fit a successful

brewery and pub into that one small and quaint building, then like its neighbours, The Rock had a secret. A long cave tunnel stretched beneath the pub and way back behind it, past its tunnel-owning neighbour Farnborough Cottages, and with two shafts to the surface. Even after the brewery ceased trading, it was used for mushroom farming and long ago attracted interest in its history and atmosphere. But you know the rest. It's under a modern block of flats now.

No.74 forms part of a short stretch of small, highly attractive old buildings. No.78 (Dorking Travel) is one of these, a modest, nicely preserved 18th or 19th century shop and house, with a cellar to match. This is entered through a trap in the shopfloor, via a short ladder. One half of it is notably low ceilinged. Down two steps it gives way to a deeper twin, lined

No.74, now the Kuoni shop, is in the centre of a stretch of densely packed, cellared old shops. Its underground brewery tunnels and mushroom farm have been lost to flats.

Above left: 78 High Street, Dorking Travel.
Far left: Cellar below number 78, complete with storage bench on three sides, and mound of sand on the floor.
Left: Long since sealed window to the street above.

on three sides with the kind of shelflike plinth typical of fruit cellars, though it is likely to have been used as well for food and bottles. Two shallow alcoves would have held candles when in use. A window up to the street has been sealed from above so long ago that no visible trace remains in the pavement overhead. The floor is thick with fine, beachlike golden sand of the kind mined at Reigate and found in only a few of the town's caves. It is sometimes called 'Shanklin sand', after its decorative kin famously collected and sold at Alum Bay on the Isle of Wight. Dig through the sand and you find the cellar is brick-floored, so it appears that the sand was turned up at some point during building and stored below, too potentially valuable to be just thrown away.

A few steps down the road, the Caveman Barbeque at 54 High Street occupies part of a three-bayed 19th century building. Below is a typical, if small, town cave cellar, reached from inside via an attractively preserved trap door next to the restaurant's front door. It appears to have been dug in two stages: a simple square, alcoved storage cellar which is likely to date back to or even before the shop's construction, then a further small, round room crudely dug out of the soft stone and entered through a rough arch.

The Caveman's cave reportedly has a sandstone-carved close relative next door at No.48. Its sunken doorway is clearly visible at the entrance to Allen Court. Unfortunately, it has not been possible to gain permission to see the cellars in the two shops that flank this courtyard. The court itself is similar to Farnborough Passage; heavily rebuilt but with one remaining old cottage. At first sight, it looks like a New

Airbricks set into the brickwork next to the road reveal cellar spaces below the pavement in front of Nos.40 and 44-46.

Town's square in miniature but in fact only one side is modern, another is old and two are very quaint. You wonder if a pop-up café and some benches would make this, like King's Head Court, a place that people go to rather than through. In 1984, a plan of the caves below one of the premises in the courtyard, No.56a High Street, was supplied to Dorking Museum. It shows really significant cellars, described as 'caves', approached down a sloping tunnel and with three joined chambers. Two pits stand nearby. The premises is now the ground floor of one of the modern blocks of flats like the ones that loom on top of Farnborough Passage and the old Rock Brewery. The caves and pits have all been lost.

As the High Street pavement rises and broadens approaching Pump Corner, it harbours cellar spaces, either buried entirely within it or communicating with ones beneath the shops. These are revealed at Nos.44-46 and 40 by squares of airbricks set into the brickwork above the road surface and by a large metal manhole cover in front of No.40 (Skipton Building Society). This hides a space below the walkway partly given over to pipework, which is kept closed. Next door, a part-glazed Victorian iron cover right in front of the entrance to Sainsbury's tops a similar, larger cellar, also holding pipework. The only entrance to it is from the pavement.

In 1968 and 1982, two handwritten lists were drawn up for the museum of the most notable of Dorking's sand caves. Both agreed that No.18 High Street was something special. However, since then even the address itself has ceased to exist.

Alongside the recent destruction of the Farnborough Passage labyrinths, the other single biggest loss of the town's underground heritage was the levelling of three cave systems, largely filled in during the 1970s construction of the Sainsbury's car park. A myth has been created about these and their sudden and dramatic destruction, including of mural-painted walls, which are described as being of possible Roman origin (despite them looking very 1960s Tolkienesque). In reality, the caves were surveyed ahead of the decision to collapse them in on themselves and two short sections were retained. There is no entrance from inside the supermarket but the council has access via a door outside. Although the council kindly helped with access to the South Street Caves and Pippbrook House, it has proved impossible to find someone who oversees or visits the other underground properties owned by them. A further well-made underground entrance at a neighbouring property leads to a small area with electricity meters and fusebox.

Thankfully, the claim that Roman murals were destroyed is as false as the story that the cellars were discovered and immediately filled with concrete. Using pre-demolition survey photos, the British Brick Society has dated the mural-painted walls to the 1960s/70s.

The premises to which the systems belonged included, at 20-28, The Chequers Inn, one of the town's earliest and largest hostelries. Now Robert Dyas, in the 19th century it was home to Mason's, a rather grand grocers and cheesemongers. Somehow, the building escaped the late 20th century cull of so many of the town's finest inns. Instead it was rebuilt with its splendid double bow-front preserved in situ. Fragments of 16th and 17th century wall paintings found during the work were saved and are on show upstairs in the shop. Beneath the attractive bow windows, barred ventilator windows to a cellar can be seen. The staff believe that it may have survived the careful rebuilding and could still be in place below the shopfloor. Any future change of fittings or layout might reveal its entrance.

78 High Street   54 High Street

70 High Street

1. Plinth
2. Alcove
3. Water tank
4. Cold room
5. Air raid shelter
6. Delivery hatch to street
7. Step

The other building that fronted the lost cellar complexes was Sauberge's, a once celebrated ironmongery, later completely rebuilt as Sainsbury's. Behind its shop, and at the Dorking Foundry on West Street (now home to Dorking Museum), goods were manufactured by a workforce of blacksmiths, whitesmiths, gunsmiths, coppersmiths and braziers. An idea of just how prolific the company was can be found in its description in Kelly's commercial directory, the Yellow Pages of its time: 'Sauberge: Furnishing & builders' ironmongers, gas fitters, smiths & bell hangers, stove and range manufacturers, agricultural implement agents & iron hurdle & wire fencing makers.' The High Street premises, like the foundry, were later occupied by Sauberge's successors, Stone & Turner, manufacturers of the fine kitchen range still to be found in the cellars at Butter Hill House.

In the 1970s, within this stretch of just sixteen premises, from Sainsbury's to No.102, nestled at least ten major historic complexes of tunnels, caves and shafts; a trove of buried treasures. Even two decades ago, many of them remained. They were an irreplaceable, fascinating warren of underground history unique to the town of Dorking. Every single one of them has been built over and destroyed. Most could have been preserved by inserting columns to support the new buildings above. Some could even have had a grating added so that residents and visitors could peer into the mysterious underworld hidden beneath the town. Instead almost every single one of these unique historic passageways to the past was filled with rubble and concrete unprotested, unpublicised and, astonishingly, without even a photo being taken.

It's a similar story for the whole length of the High Street's south side, not just this one densely packed section of destroyed historical riches. The picturesque jumble of alleys, courts, stables, privvies and outhouses that until recently used to squat behind the road's entire length has been replaced by modern flats, parking and Lyons Court road. In 2017, a sinkhole appeared here, a likely reminder of the multitude of tunnels and cellars carved out centuries before the coming of heavy delivery lorries and cars. Another emerged in Falkland Road in 2018. In recent decades, potholes in two main town centre roads have been filled, then reappeared and been refilled, suggesting the existence of further voids below the tarmac. These are now even more routine than they were in 1909, when the *Dorking Advertiser* reported that 'Dorking Council has offered Mr Brown, without prejudice, £3 for injuries to his horse caused through a collapse of the surface of Moores Road'. In 1930, they thought they had solved the problem. The *Surrey Mirror* reported: 'Eighteen hundred square yards of reinforced concrete, eight inches thick, is to replace the present tarmacadam surface of Dorking's High Street, from Pump-corner to the Red Lion Hotel. A large part of the town is built on sand, not the firmest of foundations at the best of times, but the position is aggravated by the fact that in many parts there are caves and tunnels in the sandstone. Some of these serve as wine cellars and others for storage, but most are unused. In consequence, roadway foundations are always giving way under the stress of modern traffic, and there has been in the past unnecessarily heavy expenditure in patching and re-conditioning High-street. It is hoped this trouble will now be at an end.'

There is a credible story that one of the shops in this run of sixteen only discovered that it had a sand cave beneath its cellar when workmen carrying out repairs in the basement fell through into the cavern underneath. Unfortunately the store has refused permission to visit and does not wish to confirm or describe what it has beneath it. In a similar incident, a West Street building had a pneumatic drill, and very nearly its operator, come crashing into its cellar during pavement resurfacing work.

Dorking's underground past is catching up with it. The increasing volume of traffic, the now routine parking on pavements and areas not intended for that purpose by ever larger cars, and the continuous building of flats in the town centre, especially in the old courts and backyards, make it certain that there will be more potholes and collapses.

CHAPTER SEVEN

Tales from the crypts

Christianity offers us one of the great symbolic divisions, understandable in the simplest of terms: above, good; below, bad. Heaven and Hell. Its best buildings strain towards the sky, drawing the eyes heavenwards. Paradoxically, many also have stygian spaces beneath. Each soaring tower and lofty, vaulted nave, lit to the glory of God by high arched windows, is likely to be twinned with a dark and hidden vault or catacomb, unlit to the eyes of man.

Dorking's parish church is St Martin's, a *Maltese Falcon* of a building; that rare thing, a remake of a remake that is actually better than the originals. Built in 1877, it visibly reaches for the sky, and replaced a short-lived, adequate but more earthbound structure only completed in 1837, which itself superseded two medieval reworkings of the first, possibly Anglo-Saxon, church on the site.

In 1974, an archaeological dig in the crypt unearthed Roman pottery sherds but failed to find traces of that relatively tiny, possibly wooden, original church, suggesting it lies beneath the uncellared Victorian chancel. The tower holds memorials and bells from former incarnations but it is in the vaults below that a treasury of reminders of nearly two millennia of occupation and worship, life and death, are concealed.

Below left: St Martin's parish church.

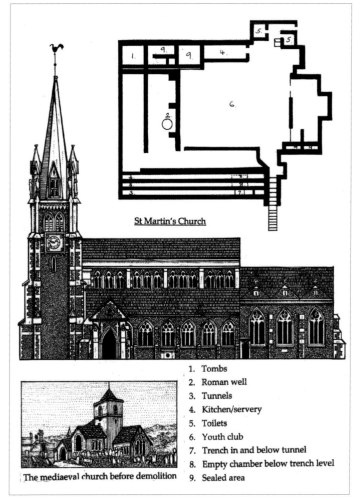

St Martin's Church

The mediaeval church before demolition

1. Tombs
2. Roman well
3. Tunnels
4. Kitchen/servery
5. Toilets
6. Youth club
7. Trench in and below tunnel
8. Empty chamber below trench level
9. Sealed area

Thanks for this are due to the now demolished first Victorian building, known as the 'intermediate church', an expensive but dumpy recognition of Dorking's increasing population and importance. Even the author of the 1855 *A Hand-Book of Dorking*, normally quick to eulogise any feature of the town, stated: 'The parish church, which was opened for divine service in 1837, has no architectural beauty to recommend it.' It did have two creditable but now lost features: its retention of part of the medieval building and a light and uncluttered interior achieved through the almost revolutionary use of cast iron columns and roof supports. It also raised the surface of the nave by seven feet (2.1 metres) to 'facilitate the formation of burial vaults' but, more importantly, to address the fact that the floor of the ancient chancel was by then six feet (1.8 metres) below its own churchyard. Worshippers had to descend sunken steps just to enter the increasingly earthbound church. The invaluable *A History of the Church and Parish of St Martin's Dorking* explains why: centuries of burials; bodies atop bodies. Until the construction of Dorking Cemetery in 1855, the graveyard had become packed not just with the remains of local parishioners and plague victims, but of soldiers billeted in the town in the Civil War, nonconformists, and the men and women brought to the town for execution. The discovery of further graves outside the churchyard itself, the book recounts, may reflect boundary theft by surrounding properties. Humanely, the corpses of suicides and the excommunicated were quietly allowed internment in the technically unhallowed ground at the yard's north side.

The church cellars concealed – and so preserved – more than just the memorials from the building's earlier incarnations (literally) unearthed in 1899 and 1974. It is not a surprise that they contain bodies. It is surprising that they also hold a genuine Roman well.

Deep, dry and lined with interlocked tiles, this is a unique survivor of a Romano-British township which was likely to have been associated with Stane Street, the Roman road from Chichester to London. The well would have served that settlement before being put into service many centuries later to provide water for baptisms (and also to fill the eighteen buckets bought in 1763 to fulfil a medieval requirement for parish churches to store municipal firefighting equipment). By then, the well was sited in the churchyard, until it was swallowed up by the building of the much larger intermediate church, which paradoxically brought this pagan, Roman-era survivor – from a time when animal sacrifices were regularly placed in wells to propitiate water spirits or gods – into the bowels of the Christian church.

The Romans were known to favour the placing of temples near springs or wells for reasons of ritual not dissimilar to the Celts who ruled before them. The early Christian church issued a number of ordinances outlawing these forms of animistic water and nature worship and moved to build on such sites. Writing in AD601, Pope Gregory described how the old beliefs still held sway among the English, who 'have been accustomed to slaughter many oxen to devils'. His solution was simple. Pagan sites should be used as churches and their idols replaced with altars. 'They should be converted from the worship of demons to the service of the true God.' In 1018, nearly five centuries after England's conversion to Christianity, King Canute enacted laws against the worship of sun and moon, trees, wells and stones. It is very possible that Dorking's parish church is where it is today because of that ancient mission to exorcise the old gods and assert the dominance of the new faith.

Beneath St Martin's lies a crypt of considerable size and, in places, confusing offshoots, tunnels, spaces and vaults. To walk in it now is to walk on the dead but also in the footsteps of the parishioners of the otherwise lost medieval church, as well as those of a more recent generation of young people.

The cellars were given new life in the 1970s as that decade's almost essential ecclesiastical feature, a subterranean youth club. Known as The Crypt, it lasted until the 1990s. It built on the example of The Cellar Club, created in 1969 by a

Above left: The well-equipped Crypt club, founded in 1973.
Above: Redolent of another decade, the unused club has a slightly Mary Celeste-like atmosphere.
Left: Beyond the youth club area is a labyrinthine collection of crypts, vaults, dead ends and blind alleys.

group of young people led by a local policeman, who cleared rubble from the large cellars and former public air raid shelter for 140 people beneath the grand gothic revival 1872 Methodist church on the corner of South Street and Vincent Road. Membership was open to 16 to 21 year olds, as long as their applications were approved by the club committee. Gambling and alcohol were prohibited, as were jeans, leather jackets and anoraks. The club, along with the huge church, was demolished in 1973, at which point St Martin's became a shared Church of England and Methodist church.

The Crypt club was particularly well equipped and has left behind a comfortably furnished communal area, with now unused pool and football tables, toilets and kitchen, as well as snapshots of changing youth interests, from discarded Abba singles to stored board games, VHS tapes and roller skates. Regrettably, it is difficult to see it being returned to its original use after a well-run family party was invaded by youths from across the county and South London when news of it leaked out on social media and the police had to be called. It's not impossible to imagine that unless things change, social historians might one day visit to see what a 20th century youth club looked like.

Beyond the club premises, through doorways, arches or holes in walls, lies a jumble of sand-floored storage rooms, tombs and tunnels, a testament to the building's many embodiments. It's a museum of St Martin's overlapping timelines. Beyond the central area, no attempt has been made to mirror the craftsmanship, finish and fine lines of the church interior above. Unwanted walls? Hack through them or forget them. No-one's

Below left: One of three crawlspace tunnels that run the length of the cellars, accidents of history and rebuilding.
Below: Marooned. An inconveniently large stone was simply left in one of the tunnels.

Above: The third tunnel has a sudden drop down to an empty tomblike space below.
Above right: An old Horsham Poultry Producers' Association box containing a 1947 Daily Mirror has somehow found its way into one of the tunnels.

going to see. A stone too large to move easily? Leave it be. Old foundations, voids and anomalies? Ignore them or brick them off. Memorial stones and graves set in the medieval floor? Bodge over them, break them up or let the sand swallow them. Three parallel, connecting flint-walled tunnels make no sense except as survivors of the earlier churches and excellent support for the floor above. Stumps of walls intrude into blind chambers. Unreachable family burial crypts are visible through holes punched into the underground walls. Masonry from an earlier building is stacked massively in a vault that also holds three 1875 gas meters which range in size from that of a small safe to a washing machine. According to an hand-penned note they were checked in March 1898 by the Dorking Gas Company. A collection of forbidden vintage light ale cans rusts away in a claustrophobic, cobwebbed crawlspace. A five foot deep trench in one tunnel reveals an arched entrance to an empty chamber below. Ancient pews are jumbled with old psalters, a wind up gramophone, pages from a 1947 Daily Mirror, a set of billiard balls, church noticeboards and broken monuments. A sundial props open a door. What lies below is a monument to the monument above.

Above right, above far right and right: Old noticeboards nestle against masonry from former churches, while tombs and monuments lie sunken into the sand.
Far right: Last inspected in March 1898, one of three redundant, cabinet-sized Victorian gas meters.

Dorking had a radical past in religion as well as in politics. In 1676, thirteen years before the Act of Toleration, the parish numbered 200 nonconformists and eighteen Roman Catholics out of 1,218 possible churchgoers, well above the national average. In 1660, Dorking Quaker Thomas Patching died in the county jail at Southwark, after being imprisoned for remaining true to the principles of his faith. By 1763, *The Gentleman's Magazine* was able to report that in Dorking 'Dissenters are numerous but live in great harmony with members of the Established Church'. In time Congregational, Methodist, Roman Catholic, Baptist and Strict Baptist churches and chapels were built, later to be joined by a Brethren chapel, a Christian Science reading room and a mosque.

In 1846, the Society of Friends constructed a meeting house on Butter Hill that had its own deep cave nearby in which fruit, coal and wood were stored. It replaced an earlier structure on West Street, also with cellar, into which an entire congregation of sixty had fallen when a rotten floor gave way. A 'corpulent fishmonger' was the first to disappear through the collapsing boards, yelling 'Stop! Stop' at the rest of the congregation who crashed down on top of and around him. They reportedly shouted back 'I wish we could!'.

A decision was later taken to quarry the Butter Hill cavern out of existence and sell the sand. This left the present building cellarless, but with one unusual below-ground feature. Before 1896, Quaker meeting houses usually had a wall-like wooden screen that allowed men and women to meet separately for business and together for worship. After that date separate meetings were ended, but by then a variety of ingenious and huge folding or rising partitions had been designed. Dorking's Quaker Meeting House is one of only two that opted for a counterbalanced bi-parting screen, one half (24 feet wide and seven high or 7.3 by 2.1 metres), complete with door, sinks into the ground, while the other rises into the ceiling space, all at the bidding of one person

Above left: Looking north in the vault housing (beneath the concrete slab in the floor) the Roman well. Through the arches are further sealed passages and tombs.
Above: Beautifully made from clay tiles, Dorking's Roman well, buried in the bowels of its parish church. The brick extension, added by later generations, shows how much lower the Roman-era land was, before two millennia of burials raised it by seven feet.

Far left: Dorking Friends Meeting House.
Left: The bi-parting screen is huge and heavy, yet the handcranked mechanism built to move it in 1846 can still be worked by one person today.

working a winch. For maintenance purposes, the deep pit into which the bottom half descends is accessible through a grating set in the floor. A drainlike tube continues below this to allow a beam attached to the screen to anchor itself below. The mechanism still works and is used to make more space for playgroup Christmas parties.

It is not known whether freedom of worship played any part in the decision by wealthy local resident and cordwainer William Mullins to join the ship Mayflower in 1620, along with his family and 200 shoes. The evidence suggests a (disastrous) economic decision rather than a religious one. Mullins was classed as one of the Strangers who funded the project, rather than the Saints who undertook it for reasons of faith. Within months of arriving in the New World he was dead, along with his wife, son and servant. One daughter survived, as did Mullins' property at 58-61 West Street, now the only known existing example of a Pilgrim Father's home.

Above right: The trap down to the pit is next to the screen half which sinks into it.
Top: In the pit. The central (of three) posts is a beam attached to the bottom of the screen.
Above: Thanks to a precisely calculated counterbalance and despite all their weight and size, the screens are moved by a simple chain mechanism.

Right: William Mullins' house stretched from what is now 58 to 61 West Street.

Built between 1568 and 1610, it was, and is, a substantial, four-gabled edifice, large enough to include a cafe, shops and flats. A recent renovation has secured its future, albeit at the expense of the cellars, which had been divided over the years as one house became four and then more. The renovation modernised, lined and smoothed them off, so that what remains is a main cellar at No.59, a small square modern one at No.60 and a cabinet sized underfloor space at No.58. The interior surface features, in particular at number 58, are well worth a look.

Behind much of the south side of the High Street there is a long, low cliff, created by successive waves of sand quarrying. Over generations, these excavations pushed it further and further back, creating swathes of space behind the original shops and dwellings which was utilised for hidden gardens, alleys, courts and backyards, stables and outhouses. Inevitably, they also shortened or destroyed some of the tunnels and caves that had been created directly behind the buildings fronting the

highway. One rare survivor is at the Baptist Chapel in Paper Mews. Nestling in the lee of the cliff, the chapel, which was built in 1910 and extended in 1960, conceals the entrance to an earlier construction, a cavern stretching back 25 feet (7.6 metres) inside the cliff. There are no records of why and when it was dug, beyond the suggestion by a local historian in the 1970s that it was probably originally approached by a 180 foot long tunnel; of this, only a short entrance stub remains, bolstered by a massive brick and cement wall and metal pipe-strengthened doorway. The solidity of the entrance wall, which includes openings for air and light, would be appropriate for an

air raid shelter but is more likely to have been intended to secure whatever was held here long before the building of the Edwardian chapel.

The cavern has one main chamber and two short offshoots, with arched, semi-domed ceilings. Interestingly, there are sixteen deep postholes set about eight feet (2.4 metres) above the sand floor, strongly suggestive of a one-time hayloft-type floor, ventilated by the openings, of which no other trace now remains. In the two stubby small chambers there are more socket holes, set lower, with cut grooves at their entrances that would accept shelving or a further floor. The mezzanines created would be too low for habitation, suggesting that the whole structure was an ambitious,

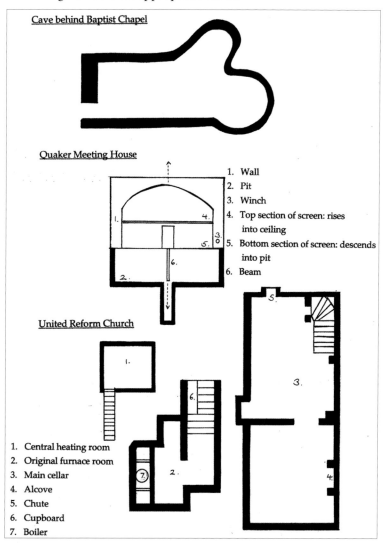

Cave behind Baptist Chapel

Quaker Meeting House

1. Wall
2. Pit
3. Winch
4. Top section of screen: rises into ceiling
5. Bottom section of screen: descends into pit
6. Beam

United Reform Church

1. Central heating room
2. Original furnace room
3. Main cellar
4. Alcove
5. Chute
6. Cupboard
7. Boiler

Above left: Dorking Baptist Chapel.
Far left: The heavily-strengthened entrance to the chapel's tunnelled cave.
Left: The arched main chamber from just inside one of the short stub rooms. Postholes set into the walls – high in the former, lower in the latter – are likely to have held wooden storage floors.

Above: The two smaller chambers, showing postholes and the heavy grooves cut in their entrances.

Below: The United Reform Church.
Below right: The main cellar.
Bottom: Main cellar, the second room.

barn-like storage facility. Sadly, its creators left behind no signature or date, unless they did but in the lost entrance tunnel down which the vault could once have been approached in perfect security.

The Congregational Church in Dorking dates back to 1662 and built its current home, the United Reform Church at 53 West Street, in 1834. The building's Italianate architecture still garners praise. Beneath the church and its associated buildings are three cellars. The largest is a double one under one of the church's public halls and the caretaker's cottage. Lit by window wells, it was used for storage and, in recent years, as a workshop.

The smallest cellar houses the central heating system. It has been modernised, insulated, lined and is as gleaming and clean as a space ship. The one it replaced is not.

The original heating cellar sits below the church interior, to which it once dispatched warm air, to be distributed through grates in the floor. It also served a network of cast iron radiators. Its boiler remains below, intact apart from its doors, with a coal bunker next to it. Once, it must have roared with flame, ever hungry for more fuel, battling to warm the much larger church and halls above. The cellar is ceilinged with slate, its walls are of brick and flint and its staircase wooden. There is none of the fine finish of the interiors above. This was a place of sweat, coal dust and iron. The stoker's original shovel still stands ready by the furnace it once fed.

Above: The furnace is still in place in the old boiler room.
Left: The furnace, with its original coal shovel.
Above: Welcome to the machine: inside the furnace.

CHAPTER EIGHT

Here runneth under

The first and fourth elements meet in profusion in the town of Dorking, as water punctures earth and stone, enabling the town's existence, enhancing its defensibility, powering its early industries and sometimes inundating it.

Dorking wouldn't be where it is without an easily accessible water supply. This it had in profusion, with a relatively shallow water table, a not wholly reliable river, and natural springs so near the surface they were practically a problem. The earliest known provision is the Roman-era well now buried within St Martin's Church. However, the real town well was the one that served the nascent Dorking from at least the Middle Ages onwards. This was sunk at the crossroads where East, West, North and South Streets meet, helping make that junction the town's beating heart, around which the medieval market grew. After centuries of use, it was replaced in 1780 by a hand-worked iron pump, giving the site the name of Pump (rather than Well) Corner. The new mechanism did away with the slow lifting of buckets to the surface, an important factor in a growing town with a thirsty livestock market and an increasing population. It seems obvious that the new public pump, the first of two in the High Street, would have been put in place over the ancient well but intuition and hearsay can make bad history. It's always worth double checking and, if you do, you'll be rewarded by finding a slab of stone with a small squared keyhole in it, a few yards from the pump. Just discernible, unnoticed and worn by centuries' of feet, is a message carved into the slab to advise future generations of what it covers. Rather thrillingly, once deciphered, it reads 'Well'.

The town was also blessed with a number of springs that were suitable for public use. The best known were at Spring Gardens and the bottom of Mill Lane, where one fed a tannery, a perennially thirsty industry whose associated pollutants were carried away by the Pipp Brook, then known as The Washway and used as rainwater runaway and virtual sewer. The 1649 manorial map shows two tanneries and a dye house there, while the site of the adjoining modern football ground in Meadowbank Park is described as a washing place. When work on the new stadium was suspended in 2017 after a spring was found below it, the only surprise was that anyone was surprised.

 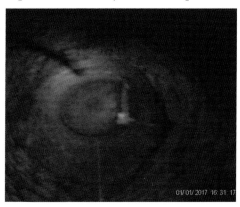

Far left: The stone that covers Dorking's town well, with its almost worn away inscription.
Left: Through the keyhole: sealed and unseen for centuries, the crudely stone-lined, 34 feet (10.4 metres) deep, medieval (possibly earlier?) well, around which the early Darkynge's town centre grew. The pipework at the bottom may have been added to feed the 1780 town pump.

The Pipp Brook at Mill Lane. Once an open sewer, it adjoins natural springs that supplied a tannery, a brewery and even the town's first piped water supply – until the sewerage seeped in.

Below: Spring Gardens, site of a public water source. Nearby, children could dig into the earth and make the water bubble out.
Below right: Spring Gardens: so pretty it's a wonder it hasn't been knocked down.

The same natural springs fed the Boxall Brewery, which replaced the tanneries and then gave way to the Evening Star pub, rebuilt in 1937 in an odd mix of styles and renamed The Malthouse in the 1980s. The building of the 20th century pub erased any traces of the tannery pits and brewery cellars but it probably occupied the void they left behind: the cellar of what is now a youth centre is unusually large. It is also so well finished in reinforced concrete that it looks like it was made ready to act as a bomb shelter, not just for the publican's family but for all the customers too.

Charles Rose noted in 1878 that 'The old Spring Gardens are all but unchanged. There is now, as there was then, and, perhaps, had been a century or two before, the old cottage close by their entrance, with the spring still issuing so strangely beneath it. Nearer the bridge, too, was a cluster of minor springs; for the spring stratum being here, so near the surface, little boys, in times gone by, amused themselves by making springs'.

William Dinnage' *Recollections of Old Dorking* were similar. He recalled: 'A spring enclosed in a small bricked cavity, down a step or two, situated close to the turning into Spring-gardens from Station-road. Another spring existed at the lower end of Mill-Lane near the old "Evening Star"'.

One valuable source of historical information is the multi-volumed *A Topographical History of Surrey*, which owed its existence to a remarkable local resident: Robert Best Ede, chemist and perfumier by Royal Warrant to the just-crowned Queen Victoria. How he achieved that commercial coup, from a tiny house in the High Street with just three back rooms, is unknown. The house was probably No.65, where a later occupant, Elizabeth Spratley, somehow managed to run, along with her husband, a hairdressers and perfumery ('Curling, Singeing, Cutting & Shampooing') while refusing to have piped water in the house. She was still drawing it from the town pump in the late 1920s.

Ede was not shy of using the royal connection in his advertising for products such as The Queen's Own Perfume, Prince Albert's Own Perfume, and Emperor of China's Perfume. Each half a crown a bottle.

He didn't stop there. In 1835, to considerable acclaim, Ede developed and marketed the first practical boxed chemistry sets for home, school and mechanics'

institute use. They were a runaway success. He announced that 'The Proprietor begs to announce in consequence, of the great increase in the sale, and at the suggestion of many of his friends, he has established A DEPOT for the convenience of the Trade and Public at 79, Bishopsgate Street Within.' Despite this, the production of the sets, of his medicines, his toiletries and perfumes, was all still being done from the rear of his High Street premises.

To support the portable laboratories, Ede published an accompanying introduction to chemistry that showed 'with what facility the principles of the science may be experimentally demonstrated at a trifling expense'. Perhaps it was the success of this that led to his next venture, the major undertaking that was the five volume *A Topographical History of Surrey*, which was typeset, printed and bound in, of course, those three small back rooms: 'It has been wholly composed and printed in his own office in Dorking'.

Born in 1798, Ede somehow packed all this into one short lifetime, dying suddenly aged 46. There is a testament to him in the *Topographical History* which seems genuinely heartfelt. Describing what later became known as the intermediate church, author William Brayley wrote: 'In a vault near the west end of the church are deposited the earthly remains of the much-esteemed and highly-lamented Mr. Robert Best Ede, the sole proprietor of this work; who, after a few weeks' severe illness, departed his life on September the 21st, 1845, in his forty-sixth year of his age. His activity and intelligence in the several occupations of a bookseller, printer, and dispensing chemist procured him many friends; and his integrity, liberal disposition, and frank and unaffected kindness, occasioned his loss to be deeply regretted by every person who had the pleasure of his acquaintance.'

Ede's tomb survived the rebuilding of St Martin's but only just. It and the little passage leading to it and other family vaults were simply bricked off and lost, their existence only accidentally revealed over a century later when a hole was punched in a crypt wall as a channel for modern cabling.

Thanks to Ede's publication, we have reliable information about a number of aspects of the town's history, including the arrival of a limited mains water supply to the town in

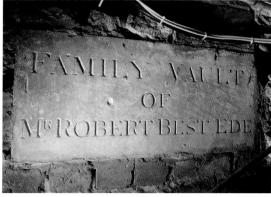

Resting place of the remarkable Robert Best Ede.

1735. It was provided by the town's first waterworks, situated in North Street. Via a waterwheel, it used the power of the Pipp Brook to pump springwater to subscribers through wooden pipes made from bored-out tree trunks, which frequently leaked and burst. (Much to the entertainment of watching children.) The *Topographical Survey* reported that 'This town is efficiently supplied with good water from a spring and water-works. On the 13th May, 1739, it was first ordered by the vestry that £30 should be expended on a water-engine for the use of the parish; and in August, 1740, a further sum was ordered to be paid for the water-engine.' Superseded in the early 19th century, the waterworks was handsomely remodelled as a private house called Brookside. In 1973, it was given a grade II listing, when it was noted that the remains of an original 'water-engine' survived in the cellars. Unfortunately, although that information is still quoted, it is no longer so. It appears that everything changed in 1985 when the building was converted into separate residences, the cellars became a flat, and the 18th century machinery was removed. Its fate is unknown.

Now known as the Old Pump House, the building displays an iron plate which states 'RP Waterworks erected 1738'. 'RP' stands for waterworks founder and Quaker Resta Patching, grandson of Thomas Patching, who had died in prison for his beliefs. His father, also Resta, had provided the town's second Friends Meeting House, into whose cellars an entire congregation later plummetted. Resta junior was eventually declared a bankrupt and imprisoned in London's grim and pestilential Fleet Prison for falsification of accounts.

By 1829, the waterworks was offering showerbaths at a shilling a go but its end was near. The Pipp Brook, by then foully choked with sewage and effluent, contaminated the spring. The millpond stank and was a town disgrace. In 1869, the Dorking Water Company was established, with a pumping station, boreholes and reservoir on Tower Hill and later on the Deepdene estate. In 1904, new boreholes and a steam-powered pumping station opened at Station Road, next to the quaintly named 'Town Destructor', Dorking's rubbish disposal furnace.

In Dorking, even the river goes underground. The River Mole has long been known for its active swallow holes, into which it partly disappears outside the town before re-emerging on the way to Leatherhead. Legendarily named for its burrowing, but actually after a watermill or mills, or for Molesey, its outlet to the River Thames, the Mole is really two rivers: one above, one below. Swallets (holes in the river banks and bed that literally swallow much of the river) have been recorded for centuries. Several were unearthed around Burford Bridge and had to be heavily capped with concrete when the Dorking bypass was constructed in the 1930s; a metal shield was also emplaced below the roundabout. The swallets also exist in the fields around the river, revealing that the second, hidden torrent doesn't just power where you'd expect it, right below its surface parent, but instead courses on its own paths, beneath the surface, boring an unexplored two-mile long cavern system of its own through the chalk.

The depth of this unentered system was dramatically proved by the 'Policeman's Hole', named after the man who witnessed its creation while shaving at his Mickleham home one morning in 1947. A snow-covered tree began waving wildly, then sank into the earth. Water welled up, then drained away. CSS recorded an attempt in 1956 to dig out the sinkhole, which had devoured the entire tree. It didn't quite manage to reach the bottom of the shaft before the expedition, led by a Miss Coleman, ran out of time, 'though it would not be difficult to reopen'. Those were perhaps, gentler times, when the Society's minimum recommendation for protective caving headgear was 'a beret stuffed with paper', but you can read a certain thwarted enthusiasm into its account: 'No one has yet succeeded in penetrating the system, although several possible places to dig suggest themselves.'

The swallow holes imbued the river with a mythic quality. In 1594 cartographer Jon Norden noted that 'at Darcking … the river goeth underground'. The legend grew when pioneering geographer William Camden repeated the story in his 1610 tome *Britannia*. In reality, there was no complete disappearance, just a change to a shallower watercourse, no matter what the maps said. Only in times of drought did the riverbed run truly dry, as it did in the unforgettable and hallucinatorily long hot summer of 1976, when it was possible to walk on the parched riverbed between the two towns. Nevertheless, the mapmakers continued for the next century to show a watercourse that turned Stygian at the town. They gave it a phrase even more evocative than Norden's: 'Here runneth under'.

Daniel Defoe railed against the myth, whose result, he wrote, was that 'many curious people have rid thither to see this place … not doubting but they should see some wonderful gulph, in which a whole river should be at once as it were bury'd alive'. Instead, he corrected, the swallows were: 'little chanels which go out on the sides of the river, where the water … trills away out of the river, and sinks insensibly into the ground. In this manner it goes away, lessening the stream for above a mile, near two, and these they call the Swallows; and the whole ground on the bank of the river, where it is flat and low, is full of these subterraneous passages; so that if on any sudden rain the river swells over the banks, it is observed not to go back into the chanel again when the flood abates, but to sink away into the earth in the meadows.'

Active swallow holes in the river bank at the left, just below the waterline.

It's a still accurate description. The swallow holes in the riverbed and banks are usually invisible beneath the surface of the water but they can be seen, slowly sucking down a twig thrown nearby, when the river is at its lowest in a long hot summer. Their older, larger brethren, whose sides have long since collapsed in on themselves, mark where the river used to flow. They can be easily seen in Burford Meadow: subsided hollows in the ground, often with bushes or a tree rooted in them, that occasionally erratically fill with water from below. The phenomenon was described in the *Topographical History*: 'In two or three of these, when the Mole is swelled by the floods of winter, the water rises by a kind of upward percolation, and is retained within them until the stream subsides, – thus evidently shewing a subterraneous communication with the river.' The book also maps swallowholes with mouths the size of barrels and mentions the appearance of sinkholes in the gardens of Burford Lodge and around Burford Bridge, a century before the 'Policeman's Hole'. The bypass builders were right to make free with the concrete.

There are more swallows in what appears to be a picture perfect oxbow lake just downstream from the rail and footbridges in Foxbury Shaw field at Westhumble. In fact, it is a meander of the river that was deliberately blocked when the railway bridge was constructed in 1867 lest it backed up the water and threatened the structure in times of flood. It is particularly visible from passing trains, sometimes full but most often dry. Yet even in the heat of summer, thanks to its subterannean secret passages, it often retains puddles of brackish water, long after there has been any rainfall to explain them.

Far left: On the hottest day of the year, the meander is like an oasis, with patches of muddy water remaining. Left: Long after the last rain, water remains.

Above: Sinkhole in the meander, its 'pipe' blocked with chalk debris.
Above right: Seen from the railway bridge it was sacrificed to protect: the former entrance to the meander, now a convenience for cows.

High above the swallows, on the steep slopes of Box Hill, two hidden, almost forgotten structures chart the days before a universal local water supply. They are water tanks built of brick on the small part that breaks the surface and of concrete within. Each had an entry hatch, whose metal doors have disappeared, either for scrap or to assuage the wartime hunger for iron.

Iceberglike, the greater part of them is below the surface; within the hillside they drop to a depth of about 25 feet (7.6 metres). Long after they must have fallen out of use, they were still dangerously full of water. To anyone peering through the doorless hatches, it might have looked inches or a few feet deep. Underground enthusiast Tony Page remembers discovering them, still filled to the top, on childhood walks in the 1970s, and his father correctly warning him that 'if you go in there you won't be coming out again'.

They appear to have provided a water supply (more regular than any the Mole could furnish) to the mansion at Burford Lodge and the fountain in its elegant gardens. The contrariness of the river would be familiar to the owners, who had a number of swallowholes in their garden. Despite the expense and the difficulty of digging, by hand, such deep excavations on a nearly vertical slope, and then pumping water to them, the tanks were placed high above the house, on the other side of the river. This is likely to have been in the early 20th century. They are virtually concealed now, as they would have been then. Perhaps this explains their existence. They are so much less visible than a high water tower that might have disfigured the gardens of the old house.

Right: Concealed water tank on Box Hill. There is an inlet pipe on the left and outflow on the right.
Far right: And its twin, also sunken into the sheer hillside.

Far left: Inlet pipe inside the tank.

Left: The tanks are around 25 feet deep. The former water level – almost to the roof – can be seen, suggesting how dangerous they would have been to enter when full, even though they would have appeared invitingly shallow.

Until very recently, Dorking was blessed with four watermills. Three outstanding ones remain: Pixham, Pippbrook and Castle mills. At the rather lovely Castle Mill on the Reigate Road two short storage tunnels, similar to those bored into the sandstone cliffs of the town centre, can be seen alongside the mill buildings.

There's been a Pippbrook Mill since at least the time of the Domesday book. The current one, on London Road, largely dates from 1792. Or sort of does: it's a faithful rebuilding after being virtually destroyed by fire in the 1970s. If that was its nadir, then its high points have been its survival and succession of uses; it has stood as a witness to both Dorking's and its own history during four centuries.

The mill had two wheels, an undershot one within the building itself and an overshot one on its north side, served by

Castle Mill

Left: Castle Mill and its short storage tunnels.

*Top row: Pippbrook Mill.
The entrance from the
millpond to the millrace.
The rectangle of light at the
very end is the observation
window below and within
the mill.*

*Second row: The millrace,
at the point where the water
disappears into and under
the mill.*

*Now dry entrance channel
to the former overshot
exterior wheel.*

*Third row:
Snail-trail-painted sluice
channel.*

*The mill pit, from outside
looking in.*

*Bottom row: A river runs
through it: observation
panel set into the mill's
entrance vestibule.*

*The nicely proportioned mill
cellars now house a meeting
room, office, kitchen and
staff area with viewing
windows.*

a now dry arched culvert. Peek over the back wall to get an idea of how this worked. Water-powered grinding ended in 1932 but the mill continued in use, mainly for storage, and in World War Two served as an Auxiliary Fire Service station, losing its cast iron wheels along the way. It was a furniture store at the time of the fire, before becoming Rhino Studios, much used in the early 1980s by The Cure. Later, Pippbrook Mill housed a publishing group. In 2011, it was sympathetically renovated as the headquarters of the Hunt Group.

In a mill whose wheel was contained within, the mill pit is the dark heart of the building. This below-ground chamber forms the lowest point, entered through a trapdoor or doorway; unlit, narrow and slippery, turbulent with the echoing rush of water. There are true stories of watermill deaths and many more manufactured as ghost stories; in several cases a miller's son or daughter fell in the millrace and was swept along by its force, perhaps knocked insensible against the gripless sides, into the clattering and merciless iron wheel. Yet, despite that, there is something special about these particular spaces, an echoing pocket of darkness, insulated from the rest of the mill, close and alive with the water's pounding and spray. So it's rather special that at Pippbrook Mill this same chamber has been imaginatively opened up to daylight and to safe viewing through three strengthened observation windows, one of which you walk over as you enter the building.

CHAPTER NINE

Beneath the law

The structures of the law were once on full display in Dorking, part of the very body of the town, so firmly enshrined in towering stone, brick and concrete that it is difficult to believe that none now remains. Even underground, where so many artefacts and constructions unexpectedly live on, few traces remain.

Once there were courts, police stations, a jail, cattle pound, stocks and, on Coldharbour Lane, a gallows, to which the condemned were whipped, tied to a waggon. Now there are none. The town's first purpose-built police station, complete with a cell on the side, was in South Street. It was long defunct by the time of its demolition in 1960, which allowed the naughty boys to enter the caves below it. Over a century before, it had replaced a town cage described by Charles Rose in the 1870s as 'the place for detention for persons no better than they ought to be'. Even before that there were cells and stocks built into the market house which was demolished in 1813. As the town grew, the South Street police station was replaced in 1894 by a grand High Street complex of the law: a courthouse, police station and superintendent's house. Puzzlingly, the two larger of these three austerely handsome buildings were demolished for office space in 1986 leaving just the smallest one, the station house, now known as the Old Courthouse, at 277 High Street. Its semi-basement is still in use, as part of the dental practice there, but the police station and court, with their cells and cellars (used as an ARP centre in World War Two) are lost forever.

The town's history was one of steadily improving facilities for law and order in line with the growth of population. Paradoxically, now Dorking is at its largest, there are none. The last police station, opened in 1938 in Moores Road, was closed in 2013 and has disappeared beneath new housing. Its replacement, a counter at the town hall, only lasted a few years, surviving a little longer than the purpose built 1960s magistrates' court at Pippbrook, which, inevitably, has been replaced by more flats.

If the physical structures of the criminal law and its enforcement have disappeared from the town, those of the civil law have not. Dorking retains a strong presence of legal practitioners. A leading example is Downs Solicitors. Their premises are deceptive, seemingly limited to an entrance and narrow frontage at 156 High Street, but in reality comprising the floors above and below the neighbouring Nos.150-154, as well as an almost secret garden behind the frontage, with, at its end, Constable Court (which has an entry at No.62 Dene Street). The High Street buildings appear to be one, but are in fact two large residences built in the first half of the 19th century, and given a shared stucco façade with matching cornices, parapets and ornamental ironwork balconies.

156 High Street, Downs Solicitors.

When in 1886 the firm's founder, J Dundas Brown, moved from his office in the arch at Rose Hill House to No.156 he would have found a large townhouse with cellars to match. Accessed from an internal staircase behind a door, they stretched from one end (probably a servants' work area and once dimly lit by now-blocked light wells), past pantries and a wine cellar, to a coal bunker below the pavement out front. The ventilator and coalhole cover for this are still evident from the street above. With the change from residence to offices, the pressing need would have been for secure document storage. This was achieved by adding a fine Victorian strongroom door to what was probably previously a cold storage larder. The whole of the sub-surface area is now given over to the keeping of files.

Above and above right: The wine and food storage areas were converted to document storage.

The same is true next door, where the original resident, a Dr Curtis, lived and practised. Downs have been a regular participant in the annual Heritage Open Days; visitors have been able to see where Dr Curtis incised his initials and hear how he had to treat the owner of a nearby house injured in an serious explosion. The neighbour had smelt gas and then 'incautiously ordered his maid servant to bring him a lighted candle'.

The cellars below the doctor's residence and consulting rooms are unexpectedly large, until you take into account the exigencies of looking after a big Victorian house and family and the sheer number of servants who had to meet them. If you look past the neat modern racks of files, you can visualise the bustling below stairs area of a large 19th century house: the stone-floored scullery, kitchen, food preparation and servants' dining areas, all in a perpetual semi-darkness leavened only by gaslight and the dim illumination of windows at the bottom of light wells, with the cold and damp kept at bay by the cooking range and fireplace. If those were the relatively warm areas, then the cold ones were on the eastern side, starting with a small windowed room that may have been the butler's pantry, then stretching below the whole side of the house

Below, left to right:
Strongroom door.
The strongroom contains a sometimes eccentric mix of files and personal effects.

in a succession of unheated, windowless larders, plus beer and winestores with arched alcoves for storage and strength. At the end, colder, lower, damper and unplastered, are three slightly dungeon-like coal cellars. These stretch below the pavement; you can clearly hear pedestrians walking and talking above, and, via a ventilation pipe, smell their cigarettes.

Just opposite Downs, the town's longest established solicitors, Hart Scales & Hodges, have occupied 159 High Street since its construction in 1782. Vague rumours of a passage under the High Street connecting the two firms can be traced to what could be mistaken for a blocked tunnel running from the sunken forecourt surrounded by railings in front of the building. In fact, this is a coal cellar that stretches below the pavement and edges under the road. It adjoins a one-time tradesmen's entrance which leads to the servants' working areas underneath this excellently preserved, elegant Georgian townhouse.

Above, left to right: One of two staircases from the garden.
Just one half of the cellars below the house.
In an Upstairs, Downstairs world, this was very much the downstairs.

Top row: Servery counter from kitchen, previously equipped with a fold down hatch. The adjoining room is likely to have housed the (removed and sealed) internal staircase to the ground floor.
Brick-floored alcoves run the length of the eastern side of the cellars.
Bottom row: Coal cellars. Looking up at the former coalhole in the bunker's arched sealing, now sealed with a condensation-covered slab of stone.

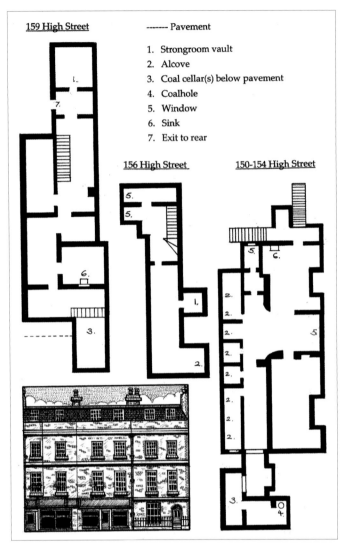

159 High Street

------- Pavement

1. Strongroom vault
2. Alcove
3. Coal cellar(s) below pavement
4. Coalhole
5. Window
6. Sink
7. Exit to rear

156 High Street   150-154 High Street

Top right: The elegant 18th century 159 and 155 High Street.

Below street level is the servants' and tradesmen's entrance. Behind the stairs is the sunken coal cellar.

Next to the basement doorway is a room with its lockable original window shutters still in place, guarding a small boxed sink with an unusual folding tap. A window in the internal wall would have afforded some feeble light to the adjoining room, probably the butler's pantry.

In the 1800s, a maid went out to the bunker and filled a coal scuttle, then returned through that door. She probably stopped while she washed the coal dust from her hands at the little lidded servants' sink. Perhaps she sighed as she picked up the heavy scuttle again and began to heave it up the stairs. Then she died. Her body was only discovered when an angry solicitor descended to berate her for not lighting the fire in his office.

The cellars contain other relics and stories of the past, as cellars often do, as well as reams of records and documents. There is a vault whose door was made by the firm of John Tann, an early and once famous safemaker. (In the 1880s they advertised that 'When Napoleon was still a Corporal, Tann was making safes'). Also kept below is the solicitor's horsehair periwig of one of the firm's founders, an artefact immediately recognisable from the illustrations of Hogarth and Gillray. It lives in the original tin in which it was supplied by JK Metherell, Law Wig & Robe Maker of Temple Bar, London.

There's something interesting next door at 155/157 High Street. In the 1970s, CSS explored below the then Chevertons shop (later Allsorts and previously Lasletts, with, for several

decades, the Orange Café above). They climbed through a hole in the cellar wall, down a bank of rubble that almost blocked a probable former staircase and into a sandstone cavern. This had two alcoves, one large, brick lined and running under the road. All inquiries and cross referencing with building plans and people who had later rented or used the cellar suggested that this mysterious

Above left: Now filled with old racking, the rather elegantly arched coal cellar stretches under the pavement and road.
Above: Original shutters at the cellar entrance, and boxed washbasin.
Far left: The boxed sink, with fold-up tap.
Left: Vault door.

deeper level had been lost and sealed off since that time. However, its entrance was rediscovered in 2016 by workmen clearing rubbish in the basement. This sounds like a classic Dorking two storey 'cave' that grabbed extra space by digging out below the highway. At time of writing, the property is still awaiting redevelopment. So far, it has not proved possible to gain permission to visit; it is to be hoped that this can be achieved in the future.

Another supposed former bastion of the law is Little Dudley House at 77 South Street. This handsome building, which still displays fine original beams and a monumental fireplace, began life as a large private residence before 1733. Among its occupiers is said to have been a judge, who reportedly presided over assizes courts there. From this sprang rumours of a cell beneath. For much of the 19th century the building housed a private boarding home for girls. It has also served as a malthouse and tea rooms. Until early this century, it was a (now fondly remembered) Italian restaurant, Pizza Piazza. At that time you could ask the staff and they'd allow you a quick peek at the historic cellars from the stairs down. Those days have gone.

Left: The court wig of one of the firm's founders…
Below: …complete with his signature, 'WJ Hodges, Esq', and the maker's label.

CHAPTER TEN
Fields of stone

For all its forests and fields, rolling hills and vales, Surrey has always been an industrial county. It was a centre of iron production from pre-Roman times until the 18th century, its deep forests offering a bounty of ore to be mined, charcoal for fuel and water power for working the great furnace bellows. It was a place alive with the clatter and din of countless watermills shaping iron and brass, sawing wood, producing wire, gunpowder, paper, corn and cloth. Now-sylvan settings such as Friday Street and Abinger Hammer would once have been lit by the blaze of furnaces and foundries and echoed to the crash of huge beam hammers pounding metal. Alongside those industries, there was the ceaseless mining and quarrying of hearthstone, firestone, building stone, gravel, iron, flint, chalk, fuller's earth and clay for brickmaking. Even the woods were relentlessly busy with the production of timber for shipbuilding, fuel, charcoal, fencing and housing. Below and among Surrey's fields and woods, up tracks and down overgrown paths, hide quarries, the traces of railway lines, spoil heaps, brickworks, crumbled workings, flattened factories, millponds and weed-choked streams once towered over by hundreds of mills, tanneries, brewers and fullers.

The town was once famous for one product: Dorking Lime. The road names give away where it was produced: Chalkpit Lane, Limeway, Chalkpit Terrace. Alongside and beneath these roads once stretched a huge quarry and towering lime kilns. It was an enormous operation that only closed in the 1940s. *A Hand-Book of Dorking* noted that: 'Dorking is especially famous for its Lime and for its Fowls. In the Chalk Pits ... are several large kilns. The lime produced here is much valued for its property of hardening under water, and it is said to have been first extensively used in the metropolis, in building the London Docks, and the Sessions House and County Gaol at Horsemonger Square.' It was also used for the Bank of England (1788 onwards), Somerset House (1801) and West India Docks (1802).

The lime was considered the best in the country, according to JS Bright, who wrote in 1872 that its quality 'created many years ago an excitement which was called the lime mania'. It became so famous that two rival works were built at nearby Betchworth, both trading on the Dorking name.

However, it was the town's quarry and works, now completely filled in and built over, that took onlookers' breath away. They almost deprived the usually verbose author of *A Picturesque Promenade around Dorking* of words to describe them. Breathlessly he talked of 'Tremendous precipices and chalk-pits which are continually wrought (and) immense kilns,' and said that they were 'by far the most extensive' of the competing concerns. If so they must have been truly spectacular; the by inference smaller but thankfully remaining works at Betchworth are still treasure troves of industrial archaeology.

These two quarries (one known as Brockham Lime Works) are well worth visiting. Betchworth Chalkpits was a huge operation, studded with great arrays of kilns and laced with four different gauges of railway track and its own sidings at Betchworth

Above: Betchworth Chalkpit's huge 1901 Smidth kiln in the foreground and the Dietz kiln behind.
Above right: Looking down and into the site's earliest surviving building.

station. Once alive with quarrying, digging and burning, and strident with the noise of blasting, trains and engines, it is now a lorry park, nature reserve and landfill site. It's also an industrial archaeology location of national importance, although almost unrecognisably reduced in recent decades.

Under the surface, especially below the diminishing number of surviving historic limeburning kilns, is an underworld of dead industries and of chambers and tunnels built beneath them. These were enlarged, rebored and adapted during their constant modernisation from the 1860s on, creating yet more vaults. The towering but never used Smidth kiln has a chamber 15 foot deep beneath it. Also below the ground, but never meant to be, are two unique Hoffmann kilns, originally with tall, slender chimneys and arched underground entrances served by the company's steam locomotives, which approached them through their own railway tunnel. These two kilns, the first of their type ever built in Britain, were buried in rubbish as part of the 1980s-1990s landfill operation. The permission to do this was given in the idealistic (or convenient) hope that this will preserve them for a later generation who will

Right: The twin towered 1880s Dietschz kilns sit on top of six 1860s kilns and are punctured beneath by their earlier chambers. Chalk was carried to the top of the chimneys by an aerial conveyor, the collapsing gantry of which still survives.
Far right: The battery of kilns once had its own railway line and platform on each side, one bringing the chalk, one taking the lime onto the national rail network. Totally overgrown, this was the platform.
Bottom left: Opened up to the air, and perilously hanging in place on rusted girders, a hopper still encrusted with solidified quicklime.
Bottom right: Inside a kiln.

Left: Under the ground below the kilns are portals, a tunnel and chambers of surprising depth.
Below left: Everywhere there are apertures, gratings and ways down.

choose to clear away the countless tonnes of decomposed refuse that entombs them, dig them out and restore them.

During World War Two, the quarry was, like many around Dorking, used as a firing range and for manouevres, the largest of which was witnessed by King George V. Live ammunition and explosives were used, resulting in two soldiers being seriously wounded, something that was accepted as the price to be paid for the realism and experience gained by the participants. Shortly afterwards, four boys took a train from Brixton and entered the prohibited area in search of souvenirs. They found one, probably a grenade. It exploded, killing one boy and terribly wounding two others. The survivor begged for help at the nearest bungalow. The occupant, Mrs Elsie King, did what she had done for the casualties of the military exercise. She quickly stripped the bedsheets and grabbed towels, then went to apply dressings and tourniquets.

In 1944, local British units destined for D-Day received fifty Churchill tanks with a new 75mm main gun. This created a problem. Did they work? Did the ammunition? It was a life and death question. To answer it meant driving the tanks long distances to firing ranges large enough to test deadly shells capable of travelling for miles. To do so would wear down tracks, engines and gears, risking potentially deadly failures in the coming combat. In a clever piece of improvisation, someone decided to use Betchworth Chalkpits instead. The tanks converged clatteringly on the quarry from miles around and test-fired their lethal loads directly into the soft chalk of its sides.

Right: The chalkpits are rich in industrial heritage. Below and below right: The site is now a nature reserve, landfill site and lorry park.

Thanks to the farsightedness of the manager of the Dorking Greystone Lime Company, Major Taylerson, some of the locomotives and track were preserved when the business finally closed in 1960. Housed at the neighbouring Brockham Lime Works, these grew into a collection that was later transferred to Sussex to form the core of the Amberley Museum Railway.

Both sites, with their huge quarries, railways, spoil heaps and profusion of kilns, were also centres of mining for a now almost forgotten product: hearthstone. This was a mineral pigment sold in bars and used to whiten stone doorsteps, windowsills and hearths. It enjoyed a century-long flowering as a must-have consumable before slowly beginning to fade out of fashion after the World War One. The centre for this relatively brief, nationwide craze was around Betchworth, Brockham, Reigate and Godstone. Dorking was, almost unbelievably, a mining town.

In 1968, CSS investigated and found traces of an unexpectedly large warren of hearthstone tunnels and shafts at Betchworth. These had begun right over the other side of Pebblecombe Hill. Named 'Cawley's Mine', they got deeper and deeper, then took a turn and headed towards and then under the huge Dorking Greystone Lime Company's site. There an adit, a new horizontal entrance shaft, was sunk in 1908 beside and below the eastern battery of kilns. CSS reported: 'A honeycomb of tunnels branches out from the main adit, and in them was laid a 19 inch gauge line, hand-worked with wooden tubs apart from the mouth of the mine, where there was a steep incline up which the wagons were hauled by a stationary engine … The airshaft to Cawley's can still be descended on Pebblecombe Hill.'

In their 1923 book *The Downs and The Sea*, Charles Harper and JC Kershaw gave a vivid picture of the mining operations, which at both sites were going on not just alongside the constant blasting, digging and limeburning in a quarry itself carved out of the rock but also under the railway lines, tunnels and kilns with their chambers upon chambers beneath them: 'These hillsides of Betchworth support, all unknown

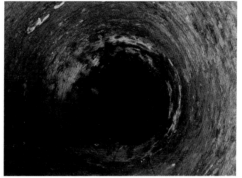

Far left: Brockham Lime Works, with the kilns, which closed in 1936, behind and the fenced vertical shaft of a hearthstone mine in the foreground.
Left: Looking into the hearthstone mine.

to the public in general, a curious small industry – that of quarrying for hearthstone. It is rather over a hundred and twenty years since hearthstone was introduced, for the purpose of whitening domestic hearths, doorsteps and window-sills. Every housewife loves a newly-whitened doorstep and a clean hearth in the kitchen; and on these domestic ideals the hearthstone-quarrying industry in maintained.'

'In the quarries owned by Messrs Blanchard at Betchworth are employed as many as fifty men: real old Surrey rustics; for largely this is a traditional occupation – son succeeding father in it. The quarry-entrance is just a small hole in the hillside, like the workings for a small tunnel, not like a mineshaft. This unimpressive entrance, however, rather astonishingly branches out, when once you enter, in all directions, for the workings have in the course of years become very extensive. They are by no means lofty; and, indeed, a tall man can scarce stand upright in them. It is cold and dark and damp within, and work is carried on by means of oil lanterns and candles. Horses are employed in pulling out the trolley-loads of stone, and are provided with great soft pads fixed to their heads, in case they throw them up in violent contact with the roof, which is liberally propped with timbers.'

The mines have been judged too dangerous to enter now, and the entrances buried,

Far left: Inside one of the lime kilns.
Left: Partial cave-in
Below left: And cave-in prevention.
Below: Surviving surface buildings.

*Right: Inside the buildings.
Note the narrow gauge
tracks in the floor.*

but at Brockham Lime Works the vertical shaft up which the stone was lifted by steam crane was conserved. It has been given a grating that allows visitors to peer down to its bottom. A crumbling tunnel leading off it to the former entrance to the mine, which opened in 1881 and finally closed in 1925, has had to be sealed.

A battery of decaying limekilns remains at the Brockham works, kept upright by scaffolding, fenced off and given over to bats (eight or more species now find their homes there). Some surface buildings, which would have held offices, an engine shed and a loading area, survive. As at its much bigger neighbour, more remains underground. According to research, apart from the mine itself, the features 'of which only below-ground archaeological evidence is likely to survive, include a stationary steam winding engine, a grinding mill, a steam crane, a coal elevator, and two wells'.

To squeeze into the collapsing kilns and tunnels at Betchworth is to enter what in the past you imagine to have been a hell of noise, heat and flesh-consuming lime, ever ready to drip onto exposed skin and coat parched throats and smarting eyes.

Paul Sowan is an expert in the marriage of geology and industry in South East England. The Brockham works is one of many sites he has lovingly recorded and helped bring back from the brink of being forgotten. By studying those records which are still available, he has established that the accident record, at least by the 20th century, was less bloody than would be expected for such an inherently hazardous environment. This appears to be in part a testament to the changes made by the successive (and heavily-resisted) waves of health and safety legislation in the 19th century. Between 1910 and 1934, nineteen accidents were recorded at this, the much smaller of the two sites. Most were from falls or being hit by falling rock. The exceptions included Arthur Clark, who was kicked by a horse, and Peter James Brannan (29), who was thrown off a waggon when it left the rails. Six of the casualties were hearthstone miners: foreman James Powell (60), Albert Henry Butcher (37), Arnold Harvey (38) (injured when a waggon left the rails 'pinching him' between it and the tunnel wall) and William Knight (47), Robert Mackrell (42) and William Cox (26) (all hurt while loading or manipulating trucks of hearthstone). It was a different story in the previous century, from which fewer records survive. In 1895 alone, there were three deaths. In April, Henry Laker (44) fell from a railway waggon and was hit by another. He died that day. In October, Eliza Gyle (75), a widow who lived in the cottage next to the works (which is still there) was killed by a railway truck. Given that the line ran through her garden and she would have crossed it daily, it has been suggested that her death might have been suicide. The same day, William Fisher (37) was shot by a colleague playing with a gun he said he believed was unloaded. It was claimed that it was kept to shoot up chimneys to clear soot.

Brockham Lime Works is now a site of special scientific interest, whose quarry, railway lines, platforms and embankments, spoil heaps, brickworks, cuttings and diggings are being softened, greened and reclaimed by nature.

Among the rolling landscape at Westhumble, not far from its ruined 12th century chapel, is a former chalk mine, a pure industrial site all the more surprising for being surrounded by lush fields and woodland. Its blockhouse entrance, specially built in 1996 to provide nesting conditions for bats, nestles in a now wholly overgrown quarry pit. To approach it is to step just a little out of the warmth of the sun; it is slightly cooler and damper than the land that surrounds it. It's possible to imagine that those who once worked there noticed that too, as they prepared to descend underground. Nature has returned and taken over but you're reminded you're on chalk and among former workings when, blithely admiring the scenery and identifying the ivy-buried sheets of rusted corrugated iron, your leg disappears knee-deep into a leaf-covered hole.

Westhumble Mine: the entrance and roosting block, part of the transformation from redundant workings to nationally important bat hibernaculum.

Little is known about the mine's history. The first identifiable reference to it used to be from 1912 but detective work by Paul Sowan has turned up a much earlier document. In 1796, Joseph Peters, who described himself as 'The original Darking lime-burner', issued a prospectus for his works at Dorking and Westhumble. It lists his prices and clearly names the Westhumble site. (Peters' claim to be the first Dorking limeburner is false. The industry was at least 173 years old even then: the parish register records the death of Myles Crowney, 'killed by a stone at the lime works at Dorking on 30th July 1623'.)

It remains uncertain whether the mined chalk was used only for lime or for building stone too. Chalk was never a good stone for construction but offered the advantages of being local and easily hewn. Its shortcomings became irrelevant if it was dedicated to interior use, for example when being hand-shaped into decorative fireplaces. However, it is not among the products listed in the prospectus, which advertises 'stone lime, small lime and small lime for land'. All burned in a kiln at Westhumble, of which not a trace survives.

Inside the mine there are none of the wide, regular tunnels seen in, for example, the building chalk mines at Guildford or the 19th century Kent mine now known as Chislehurst

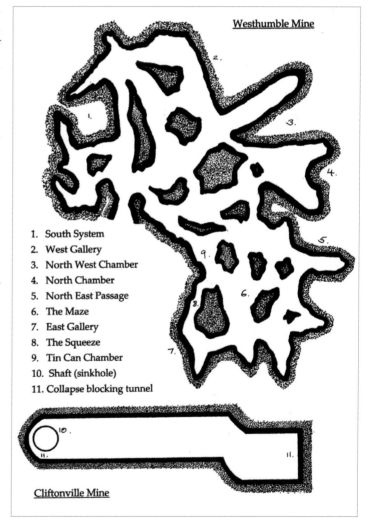

Westhumble Mine

1. South System
2. West Gallery
3. North West Chamber
4. North Chamber
5. North East Passage
6. The Maze
7. East Gallery
8. The Squeeze
9. Tin Can Chamber
10. Shaft (sinkhole)
11. Collapse blocking tunnel

Cliftonville Mine

Right: Westhumble Mine, a living reminder of Dorking's unexpectedly rich mining history.
Far right: Mined chamber with (illuminated) an entrance to the next one.

Caves. Instead there are chambers, each dug until exhausted, when the work moved on to the next. Even allowing for rockfalls the connections between them are obstructed by piles of waste and undug stone. The workmen would have had to scramble over piles of rock to get from one chamber to the next. This explains the names of sections such as 'The Squeeze' and 'The Maze'. There are no rails and no evidence of pit ponies. Once dug, the chalk would have had to be laboriously carried out by hand. For all its serpentine ramblings in pursuit of product, this looks like a tough, long lasting but relatively small operation when compared with the vast works at Dorking and Betchworth.

The ceilings and walls still show the marks of pickaxes and hand tools, the pitted tracings of years of hard, ill-lit, dangerous and noisy labour. Maybe unbearably noisy: the stone would have echoed and re-echoed maddeningly with the crash of metal on metal and metal on rock. Piles of unsuitable stone have been stacked into insecure walls. Here and there are fallen pit props that would once have given a little protection against the risk of cave-ins in this most unstable and dangerous of rocks to mine. Then as now, the damp chalk glistens and slips and can break underfoot.

The mine is now massively barred but, before it was secured, entering its tunnels was, like the Deepdene bunker, a rite of passage for local boys, despite its periodically flooding. In 1963, CSS noted: 'Considerable breakdown has occurred … more care should be taken than at other locations. Some years ago a boy was trapped for eight hours when an entrance he was digging out collapsed on him. He was rescued eventually by firemen.' The Society approvingly noted that he had gone on to become one its members.

On a recent tour of the South Street Caves, a visitor gave a typical account of exploring the mine. As a young boy he went in, unwillingly, as a result of peer pressure, on an expedition carefully kept from parents' ears. It was cold and confusing, it was wet. They had to crawl over slippery and crumbling rockfalls. Eventually he emerged, rather proud of himself for surviving and not losing face. He went home a hero to

Below: Pickmarked ceiling and walls.
Below right: Spoil – stone that is too small or too weak to be of use – heaped into a wall.

himself, too happy to notice that from head to foot he was plastered with chalk. His mother gave him a beating for it.

The mine is on land owned by the National Trust, which leases the caverns to the Surrey Wildlife Trust. Under the careful stewardship of the Surrey Bat Group it is now recognised as a bat habitat of

national and international importance. Among its occupants are Bechstein's Bat, one of the UK's rarest mammals, thought to number just 1,500 in the British Isles.

Despite this, it was broken into by some particularly ridiculous 'ghost hunters' in 2017 and then by a group who describe themselves as 'urban explorers'. After seriously disturbing the roosting bats and damaging the protective bars so badly that the entrance was unusable for months, they posted the film of themselves walking around the 'Dorking salt mine' (sic) on YouTube. Others followed. Over the last few years, they have cut the bars with an angle grinder, attacked the doorway surround and hammered the locks out of existence. In August 2018, unbelievably, they went even further and painstakingly destroyed all the nesting boxes in the purpose-built roosting areas.

One Dorking underground industry that had a much shorter life was discovered when a proprietor was chatting outside his High Street premises with a police officer and she asked 'What's that smell?'. On investigating they found that his locked cellar had been dug into from an adjoining premises and a cannabis factory installed.

in 2015, an alarming discovery in a children's play area left a homeowner with a desirable historical artefact buried below his garden and some unanswered questions. Cliftonville is a road of elegant, mostly Victorian, villas. The owners of one of them were removing their children's playhouse, which sat next to a much-used slide and swing. They noticed that the ground was oddly spongy and then that there was a hole opening up in it, which had only been stitched together by the roots of a nearby tree. They called in the Wealden Cave and Mine Society, who do such excellent work in opening Reigate's Caves to the public; they discovered a section of a forgotten and unrecorded mine, standing on its head the usual rule of thumb that Dorking quarried for sand and Reigate mined it.

Its date of origin is unknown and there are no easy clues. Square iron nails driven into the walls in two places could be from any year from 1800 onwards. The graffiti (TCH, J Caird, FHA) lacks a date, apart from a possible '1887' with the 1 missing, but that could equally be a record of volumes of sand shifted. It is certain that any work would have ceased, and maybe been concealed, by the time the houses were first put on sale in 1891.

Top: Looking down the twin barrels of the mine entrance. Outside, work goes on to repair the damage caused by forced entries.
Middle: From mine to bat cave, Westhumble Mine is a hidden survivor of a lost industrial past.
Bottom: Pitprops would once have been a vital part of staying alive while mining the chalk.

This is no folly or storage cave but a professional operation, mining sand or sandstone for sale or for building materials for the 1890s houses, or for two earlier and now demolished 19th century mansions nearby. So why not simply dig from the surface? Perhaps it was to avoid spoiling someone's view. Maybe it wasn't fully legal. Having announced its presence by nearly swallowing a wendy house (not to mention the children playing in it), the mine offers no answers.

It's a reminder of the paradoxical nature of the material on which much of Dorking sits. Leave it alone and it'll leave you alone. Mess with it and it's a different story. Handle it one way and you hold stone; another and you hold sand. As Paul Sowan explains, 'Folkestone Sand' is classified by engineers as being on the borderline between engineering soil and engineering rock. It contains little or no mineral cement to hold it together. Instead, it is technically a 'locked sand'. This suggests another possible answer to why it was mined rather than quarried at Cliftonville. Although it looks the same as in the South Street Caves, it has been tentatively identified as not actually being Folkestone Sand but a geologically older bed perhaps best accessed by following its subterranean seam.

From the bottom of the shaft, over a mound of that fallen sand, you enter a tunnel that runs 30 feet (9.1 metres) before it makes a neat dogleg and then continues for a shorter length, ending in a collapse. The tidy pickmarks of its makers line the walls and it is comfortably high. Lighting was by candles mounted on spikes driven into the stone and later removed, probably as the work progressed, rather than by the candle alcoves typical of other caves in the town to which workers regularly returned. It seems certain that the tunnel continued on at both ends; the current way in is unlikely to have been the intended entrance. Fortunately, this would take it away from any houses and instead below the bottom of people's gardens, in two of which there have been collapses, including an ornamental urn sinking into the earth.

History repeats itself. Something similar but even more dangerous happened in 1881. The *Surrey Mirror* covered the story: 'A most serious fall of earth took place in a garden skirting Back-alley[2]. It seems that excavation of sand has been carried on for a

Top: Upper floor of the roosting block. The debris is shattered roosting boxes. Above: Smashed roosting box.

Right: The hole that opened up in someone's garden. Far right: And the view from inside it.

[2] Now Church Street.

considerable time by Messrs. Salter and Baxter for which four men were engaged on Thursday. Several small slips occurring, the men became alarmed, and made for the top. They had not long been in safety before a large portion of the top of the cave fell in, making a huge gap of some 40 feet deep.'

Top left: A mound of sand stretches from the shaft bottom into the tunnel.
Above middle: Looking into the tunnel from the mound.
Top: The tunnel, with arch through to the dogleg at its end.

Far left: Tree roots have invaded the mine.
Middle: Dog leg arch…
Left: …and from the other side.
Bottom left: The collapse which blocks the tunnel.

CHAPTER ELEVEN

Taverns in the town

Dorking always had a disproportionate number of inns, pubs and beer houses: forty or more in the 18th and 19th centuries, in startling proximity. Pubs with pubs opposite, pubs next door, pubs one door down. The explanation lies in its history as a coaching stop and a market town, whose hostelries offered entertainment, food, drink and beds to farmers selling and buying livestock, and also a place where those transactions could be done on the quiet, away from the market and its duties on sales.

The market, or markets to be more exact (corn, cattle, poultry and general) created a need for convenient storage for wholesale and retail goods, as well as the food and drink necessary to service the appetites of those who bought and sold. The soft rock was a gift. There wasn't a pub in the town that didn't have a substantial cellar below it.

So it's not a surprise that the fourth largest known underground site in Dorking is below what was The Wheatsheaf, at 37-39 High Street. Built c.1450, The Wheatsheaf was a landmark inn, a genuine medieval survivor. Only closed as licensed premises in the 1970s, it was then strengthened and conserved, a little treasure whose frontage enriches the High Street, a stubby white molar flanked by the incisors of its higher, squarer, Georgian- and Victorian-façaded neighbours.

Below left: The 16th century former Wheatsheaf Inn.

It's built on several levels, up creaking steps and over wooden floors; below them, too. A small door in the one-time public bar

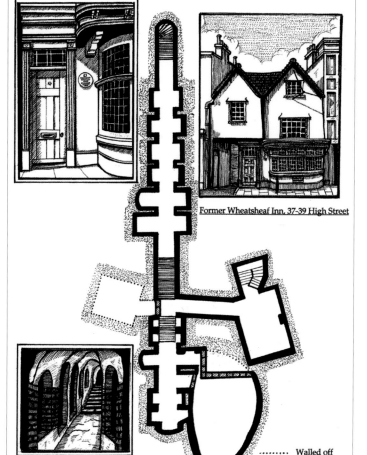

Former Wheatsheaf Inn, 37-39 High Street

·········· Walled off

descends to a roomy cellar, plus its sister basement, now walled up (though visible through airbricks) during that efficient 1970s restoration

Then there's a layer below that. A deeper one, sloping slightly downwards. Two tunnels branch away from each other, each with its own steep and partially decayed staircase (one with twenty-seven narrow steps, the other with thirteen wider ones). These corridors, each with multiple bays for holding bottles crudely and deeply gouged out of their sides, head in opposite directions: one towards the former yard, outhouses and stables, the other out under the High Street.

It's an atmospheric little labyrinth, with that instantly recognisable feel and smell of somewhere closed and very rarely visited. It also holds a rather dark little secret, a deep-buried arena where cockerels were set to fight to the death for the enjoyment of spectators.

Cockfighting, bull- and bear-baiting were outlawed by the 1835 Cruelty to Animals Act, so it would be reasonable to assume that this cockpit dates from well

Top: Stairs and bays below the former Wheatsheaf Inn. The sand is finer and more golden than in the South Street Caves.
Above, left to right: One of many bays for holding bottles.
The heavily bayed and alcoved tunnels run in opposite directions.

before then. Logic says it would have been a public area, an asset to the pub that would draw in customers, as openly on show as its skittle alley. Yet it's not where you'd expect it: behind the premises or just below them. Instead, those wishing to enter had to stoop through two small doors, descend two flights of stairs, slip into what appears to be just another wine bin and then squeeze in (the entrance is even more concealed now, as a modern structural wall narrows it and sits on top of the one-time sandstone benches). At this point, the pub below is practically as deep as the one above is high. It feels hidden. It feels furtive.

We know from the brilliant reforming Victorian journalist Henry Mayhew that clandestine blood sports continued in pubs after the Act. '(Dog) fights take place on the sly – the tap-room or back-yard of a beershop,' he wrote, 'the police being carefully kept from the spot'. However, what really rushed in to fill the gap was the sordid but then legal practice of rat fighting: setting dogs to kill scores of rats within a minute. Mayhew counted forty or more taverns in the capital offering the spectacle. He described a typical rat pit in his 1851 book *London Labour and the London Poor*

Above left: Passageway on the cockpit side of the Wheatsheaf tunnels.
Above middle: Former cockpit entrance, from inside.
Above: Decayed remains of the spectators' wooden seating
Left: The cockpit. The old piping may be from an early gaslight. Gas arrived in Dorking a year before cockfighting was outlawed.

as being 'a small circus, some feet in diameter … fitted with a high wooden rim that reaches to elbow height. Over it the branches of a gas lamp are arranged, which light up the white painted floor, and every part of the little arena … the audience generally clambered upon the tables and forms, or hung over the sides of the pit itself'.

Was this Dorking fighting pit a public facility abandoned in or before 1835 or was it, as CSS suspected, hidden and illegal? There is no obvious physical evidence. The fallen beams that once held the banks of seating are now turned cardboard-light by the damp; still formidable from the outside but inside as crumbling as the sand that lies deep on the arena floor. A niche in the wall might have held a trophy or an oil lamp. If so, its wick was always well trimmed, as there is no soot there or anywhere else. Perhaps the pit was lit by gas, which arrived in the town in 1834. Oddly, or maybe suspiciously, no customers seem to have left their names in the easily-carved walls. What graffiti there is dates from the early 20th century.

Nor are any clues given by a notice of sale of lease published in the *London Gazette* in 1867. This followed the death of owner, John Maybank, head of another of the town's substantial wine and spirit merchants. On offer above ground were the Wheatsheaf's 'fixtures, goodwill, licences, commercial room, bar, bar parlour, public parlour, tap-room, two soldiers'-rooms, brewery, store-room, granary, brewhouse-yard, billiard-room, coach-house, stable, covered skittleground and productive garden'. Below ground was a 'Basement very extensive, lofty cellarage, and two ranges of natural arched vaults of even temperature both in summer and winter'. Any mention of the pit below the arched vaults is conspicuously absent.

(Thanks to the Lost Pubs Project we know what happened to John Pimlott Brearley, who bought the lease. Three years later he was declared bankrupt. A year after that he was a prisoner of Essex County Gaol. He died in 1899, aged 53.)

Pitch black and empty, it is difficult now to imagine the cockpit as a place of entertainment: loud and raucous, thick with the fug of pipes and sweat and wet

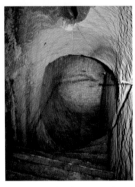

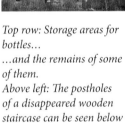

Top row: Storage areas for bottles...
...and the remains of some of them.
Above left: The postholes of a disappeared wooden staircase can be seen below the brick stairs they once led to.
Above middle: Standing where the wooden staircase used to, and looking up to a ventilation hole and one-time goods entrance two storeys above.
Above right: The tunnels below the Wheatsheaf, the cause of a minor political scandal.

with the slops of beer and cider. The hand-carved tunnels are all the more interesting for being so little visited; not forgotten but not now opened to the light. Unusable as a modern workplace for health and safety reasons, they cannot be visited by the general public without the installation of handrails and new stairs and everything that might spoil their character. Being shut away has preserved them.

There is an odd little postscript to the cellars' history. On September 13th 1884 *The Surrey Mirror* reported that 'The Surveyor drew the attention of the Board to the existence of a cave beneath the High Street from which sand was continually being abstracted and suggested that measures be taken to prevent it so as to secure the safety of the public over the thoroughfare in front of the Wheatsheaf Inn'. Did the inn's owner have a right to undermine the highway, the board asked, to which the answer was that it was 'generally understood that they claimed half way of the road'. Faced with this surprising assertion, the board decided it was unable to take any action beyond warning the owner that he would be liable if anything happened. The surveyor noted that there was 15 feet (4.6 metres) of earth between the cave's ceilings and the road's foundations, but he 'should not like to trust traction engines going over it'.

Was the digging to increase the storage space or to extract sand for profit or use? The sand in the cockpit is noticeably fine, finer than that taken from many of the town's quarries. It was certainly as good as that sold at the time as a floor covering for pubs, a hygienic way of soaking up the slops, spit and mud that, unlike the alternative straw or sawdust, didn't harbour rats, mice, mites and more. Its ability to soak up blood and fowl flesh would already have been demonstrated within the inn's premises.

That was exactly what the landlord claimed when, in fighting mood, he replied, via his solicitors, 'that it was not true that excavations were being made, and that during the time Mr. Selman had been at the Wheatsheaf no sand had been taken from the cave, except what he himself used for strewing his floor and cleaning the pots'. He also wrote to the board and angrily confronted the surveyor, HS Mathews, in his own office. It seems that Mathews had reliable information not just that sand was being dug but to whom it was being sold and for how much. Unfortunately, the information had been gained, probably unattributably, when he entered the inn's cellars without permission, accompanying a party surveying for the town's new sewers. To make matters worse, he had taken two board members, one its chairman, with him. The 'annoyed and aggrieved' landlord threatened that unless 'he received an apology and the objectionable statements were withdrawn in a public manner he should be obliged, in justice to himself, to take steps to enforce it'.

The surveyor put up a good defence: 'He had a right, where the health or safety of the inhabitants was concerned, to do what he had done. In this case he thought the safety of the inhabitants was concerned, and he thought so still. He did ask the Chairman and Mr. Todman to go down to the cave, and then they saw what sand was there. He understood that the sand was sold at the price he said; and, as to the right of going down, he thought he was justified, and also in taking any assistance he thought necessary.' However, reading the reports, you can feel the other board members edging away from him. The coup de grace came from the chairman, who was clearly embarrassed by his involvement in the unauthorised cellar expedition. He told the meeting: 'I very innocently went down, thinking the Surveyor had permission from Mr. Selman, and I had not the slightest idea that I was trespassing, or anything of the kind.' The meeting left the landlord free to do whatever he wanted: 'If he continued to excavate under the High-street he did so at his own risk. There was no imputation at all upon Mr. Selman … The matter then dropped.'

The incident reveals a curious facet of local history, a folk belief that owners could freely dig to a halfway point under the town's main roads. Many did, happily venturing part way under pavements and roadways, although there are, so far, no confirmed tunnels that completely traverse the town's roads.

There is a single-source, anecdotal and modern story that a tunnel once crossed beneath West Street from Nos.9-10, the former Rose and Crown pub, to No.55, now Viva Restaurant. Supposedly, it connected the tavern to a brothel opposite. No evidence for this has been presented. It seems unlikely that the police, who closely monitored the town's pubs, would be unaware of a regular promenade of prostitution literally beneath their noses or that anyone wishing to run a clandestine bordello would physically link it to any inn, the class of business most closely and regularly inspected by the authorities. This particularly applies to the Rose and Crown, the roughest, dirtiest and most disreputable pub in the town. It had been converted in the 19th century from two 16th century cottages into a pub and a (packed) common lodging house, with stabling for just two horses and cramped accommodation. According to contemporary records, its customers were mainly vagrants and tramps.

Number 55. No tunnel here.

Was there even a tunnel at all? Regrettably, it has not been possible to inspect the former pub cellar but Viva has kindly allowed access to theirs. It is a joined double basement. At each end there is a low and antique staircase. The indications are that the space began as two similar cellars, constructed at the same time as the building above and later joined together. Visited on one of the year's hottest days, they were cool and clean, a reminder of just why cellars were dug: they offer the perfect place to keep food and drink. The only thing missing is any closed over doorway. The wall fronting the road is unbroken, apart from a former hatch down from the pavement. It appears that it may have been this innocent niche that has been turned by someone's imagination into the lurid modern myth of the punters' passage.

These were far from being the only conjoined cellars, even if the prime examples on the High Street have been lost. Some must have been planned, others may have arisen from accidentally driving through into a neighbour's cave, at which point the two parties seem to generally have either walled up the gap, agreed a common use, or sealed one entrance and given the dual cave over to a single owner. In 1880, the *Surrey Mirror* noted that the town was 'intersected by numerous deep and winding caves'.

JS Bright, in his 1876 book *Dorking, a History of the Town*, notes that the many sand caves in the town 'are large and convenient for the storage of wine, beer, and other articles of consumption. They extend, in some cases under the public streets, and run far back into the hilly sides of the town'. The joining of tunnels might have assisted loading and unloading and moving goods from storage to stall at busy times such as market and processional days, as well as providing protection from the weather and eliminating the need to venture onto the town's notoriously muddy main roads.

In the village of Dunster in Somerset one long terrace of houses had doors added between each premises during a 17th century plague epidemic so that their length could be walked without stepping into the street. It's not inconceivable that something similar happened here (even if the greater danger might have been the day-long, town-wide affray of the town's football match).

On the subject of epidemics of pestilence, Bright noted that 'the visitation of the plague was felt frequently in Dorking', with 108 deaths in 1603 alone, many 'buried in their houses or neighbouring fields'. There may be some surprises awaiting those carrying out building work.

The enviably roomy antique cellars of 17th century, Georgian-fronted Talbot House at 51-52 West Street were home to a servicemen's and women's' jazz club in World War Two and feature what looks very much like a closed-off tunnel reaching out under the road. Entered, it reveals instead a small aperture up to an iron cover in the pavement above that confirms it as a one-time coal or wood bunker.

It's worth remembering the caution voiced by Surrey historian Mathew Alexander: 'It is not unlikely that many of these rumours (of lost or sealed tunnels) are started by wine-bins. These are alcoves built into the walls of many Georgian and Victorian cellars. They often take the form of a shallow, arched tunnel leading off the cellar, and often are only a few feet deep with a rear wall of brick. It is easy to see how these could give the impression of a blocked-off tunnel.'

Below: Talbot House, 51-52 West Street.
Below middle: Talbot House cellar, once a smoke-filled, naturally blacked-out part of a wartime jazz underworld.
Below right: Talbot House: storage alcoves.

The warrens under the White Horse and Wheatsheaf were rivalled in complexity and size by the Sun Inn at 123 High Street, which was demolished in the 1970s. This modestly sized little pub concealed a labyrinth beneath it. An 1862 auction notice described it as: 'A Beer House containing Capital Trade & Domestic Accommodations and possessing Capacious and Very Extensive Cellarage Excavated from the solid Sand Rock'. Those cellars explain why, in Dorking and elsewhere, the word 'cave'

The deceptive bay, which appears to be a blocked tunnel – but isn't.

for so long made sense when applied to man-made cellars: the rounded subterranean passages contained not just storage for barrels and bottles, but also a shooting range and meeting rooms used by clubs, friendly societies and masons. Although much of the space is believed to remain, now punctured by columns to support the building above, entry through the one remaining hatch would be so disruptive as to be nearly impossible.

The Sun was virtually sandwiched between two more inns, the Three Tuns and the Black Horse. Then as now, every pub in the town had its own character and characters, practices and functions. In the case of the Three Tuns, this included serving as an essential adjunct of the town's corn market. On trading days, its floor would lie beneath a thick coating of corn, pitched there by traders so that its quality could be judged. Outside was a long bench running along its frontage, where customers and the public could sit. In front of this Dorking's rat catcher drummed up trade by shouting out 'Death to rats!'. Others in attendance, according to Charles Rose, were a gaunt-looking man who cut hair in the open air, and 'poor blind Tom, who showed wonderful ability' in his basket work.

In 1914, the old pub moved a couple of doors down, being rebuilt in a larger and fancier form on the Black Horse site. That incarnation lasted just 51 years. The modest, twin-gabled, slightly tumbledown original, once a hub of market day entertainment, was demolished and replaced by a new shop, and faded into history. Except that it didn't quite. It appears that the cellars weren't destroyed and remained down there, below 125-129 High Street (now WH Smith). In 1991, they were described in *Dorking: A Surrey Market Town through Twenty Centuries*: 'There are two rectangular rooms with arched roofs, rather reminiscent of Nissen huts, which were used for meetings of the otherwise unrecorded Sparrow Club in the 19th Century.' Since then there appears to have been some form of rationalisation or sealing off. The current shop's cellar is described as being square, flat ceilinged and featureless.

The Ram Inn, at 176 High Street, was knocked down in 1957. It was another quite small establishment on the surface, with a reportedly much larger footprint below it. Its cellars and sand cave, along with those of the quaint old cottage shops that neighboured it, are now lost below the modern buildings installed above them.

With the coming of the railways and the ending of stagecoach routes the number of inns fell, and continued to do so as the farmers' market declined throughout the 20th century. Over the years the evocatively named losses have included The Pig in String, Great Bell Inn, Cardinal's Hat, Ram, Rock, Gun, Sun, Fox, Nag's Head, Evening Star, Market House, Three Jars and Red Lion (from whose steps the Riot Act was read in 1830, before the cavalry were let loose upon a crowd of agricultural labourers chanting 'Blood or Bread' in protest at the starvation wages then being paid). Thankfully the town still supports some fine examples of historic pubs. Of the lost ones, some buildings remain in retail or business use, with their underground areas intact.

Among the surviving hostelries is the Old House at Home at 24 West Street. Converted from cottages into a pub in 1855, it has successfully reinvented itself in recent years, not least by adding the genuinely charming Narnia Room, which is entered through a wardrobe. The pub's cement-floored cellar comprises three areas. All lined, all in use, busy with the crisp coolness of the air conditioning and the rhythmic sighs and exhalations of pumps. During World War Two an air raid shelter was incorporated. This small, low, undoubtedly cramped refuge lies at the end of the cellars, its presence now revealed only by the concrete and girder strengthening of its ceiling (which means you have to stoop to stand up in it) and by a former ventilation pipe to the surface.

The Star, at 36 West Street, is Dorking's arty pub, with a pleasingly bohemian atmosphere that goes back at least as far as the 1930s and its time as the favourite hostelry of film actor and local resident Leslie Howard and his visitors from the world of the arts. Access below is through a trapdoor behind the bar. A ladder leads down into a cellar in three sections, with a vintage barrel ramp still in use and an interesting cavity where the brick wall has literally been hacked out to create a rough niche. This is a working basement, clean, air conditioned and whitewashed, but still structurally in keeping with its early 19th century origins, and a place that, despite the modern equipment, would not seem wholly alien to its many generations of former pub staff. It is not a surprise that the managers of the Star and the Old House are keenly interested in local history.

The safest place to be in a collapsing house is under the stairs, as proved by all those wartime photos of bombed buildings whose floors have disappeared but whose staircases remain, eerily climbing the surviving walls. Below The Cricketers at 81 South Street is another clean working cellar, enclosed by the brick walls of the attractive, tilehung early 19th century building. Below the stairs and just off a short corridor leading to it is a small room whose girder- and concrete-reinforced ceiling suggests

Right: The Star (left) and Old House at Home (right). Far right: The air raid shelter in the Old House at Home's cellar, showing its low reinforced ceiling, complete with ventilation hole at right.

that it served as an air raid shelter for the owners. Whether they felt tied to the pumps by customers who didn't immediately heed the sirens or whether they calculated that the public basement shelter below the Dorking Book Shop (where Waitrose now stands) was too far to get to in time, they made the decision to significantly strengthen one area against the danger from above.

Above left: One of the cellars at The Star.
Above middle: Cavity gouged out of the cellar wall.
Above: Original barrel ramp.

The story of the historic cellars of the 19th century White Hart pub at 5 Dene Street (formerly known as Ram Alley, after the Ram Inn) is one of thwarted attempts to use them or to allow customers to enjoy them. Just as the current landlord, Andrew Mitchell, arrived in 1987, the authorities ruled that the cavernous stone cave could not be used to store drink, as the walls were unlined. The brewery disagreed and pointed out that for centuries the town's caves had been safely keeping beer at the optimum temperature. Plus, tellingly, that the pub was allowed to sell wine and champagne which, famously, is fermented and stored in identical conditions. No one was listening. To line the caves would involve high costs, lowering the floor, and positioning a skip that would inevitably block the roadway. In the end, one section of the old cellar was lined and extended and the rest walled off and left empty. Andrew Mitchell then gated one half of the cave cellar for customers' use but this too was prohibited.

What remains now is effectively three interlinked cellars that were once one. First the modernised area, with a great oaken beam still set in the ceiling. Then a deep, hand-carved sandstone chamber, alcoved, arched and part-flagstoned. It would once have held scores of barrels of beer and cider. Near its entrance, it gives onto a smaller, now separate walled space, which was going to be for customer use.

This part would once have been deep and dark but has now been made visible by creating a small gated entrance in the wall of what was the gents' toilets, which were converted into a small backyard smoking area. (The story of why the replacement toilets have a police box front is told in the invaluable *Time Gentlemen Please: the Story of Dorking Pubs*). If you visit before 9pm, you can look in through the bars; a torch will help.

Below left: The Cricketers
Below middle: The cellar at The Cricketers.
Below: Former bomb shelter room with heavily reinforced ceiling.

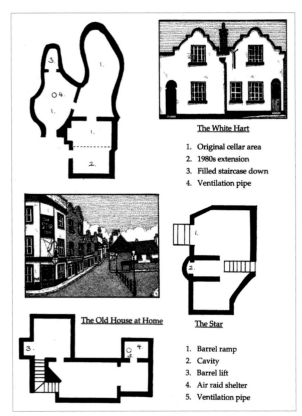

The White Hart

1. Original cellar area
2. 1980s extension
3. Filled staircase down
4. Ventilation pipe

The Old House at Home

The Star

1. Barrel ramp
2. Cavity
3. Barrel lift
4. Air raid shelter
5. Ventilation pipe

Above right: The White Hart.

Inside, on the right, is a gate to the larger cellar, and straight ahead is an intriguing further stub, full to floor level with sand (and in 1987 with broken furniture, coal and years' worth of fireplace ashes). This is very clearly a one-time staircase down to a further level: either a rumoured but unlikely passage to the 16th century Surrey Yeoman pub on the High Street, which is said to have collapsed in the 1970s, or, more likely, a further, deeper, stone-carved chamber.

Framed in the bar is an 1849 advertisement for an auction, to be held at the Wheatsheaf Inn, of the 'White Hart Licensed Victualling House', complete with a 'good bar, tap room and parlour, and a cellar excavated from the Rock and capable of extension without expense'. It also notes: 'There is a Well of fine Spring Water on the Premises, used by the Tenants in common.' This too may now lie beneath the floors of the cellars.

The Surrey Yeoman, at 220-222 High Street is one of the town's oldest pubs. Its timber-framed building was remodelled in Victorian times and quietly modernised

Right: View into the smallest of the White Hart's three cellars from the gate in the smoking area (open until 9pm).
Far right: The small cellar, with a cavity on the left wall that goes several yards into the rock, and the sunken staircase on the right.
Bottom left: The gate and wall added to allow this space to be used by the public.
Far left: Filled-in staircase to a deeper level passage, cave or well.

Above left: The largest section of the cellar.
Above middle: At its end, golden sand and space for barrels.
Above: Old brick and flint work and alcove.
Far left: Alcove for bottles.
Left: Looking back towards the current cellar. Note the old flagstones.

many times since. As above, so below: the two-room cellar hints at its age with candle alcoves and recesses, but includes much later additions such as a metal ladder, brieze block walling and a cement floor that now limits the headroom. Two apparent bottle bays are suspiciously shallow, suggesting infilling, while a large arch could be a support for the structure above but could possibly also have served as a doorway to a further cellar room or a proper staircase up. There is no evidence of any tunnel to the White Hart.

Even a comparatively simple cellar conceals clues. No.13 High Street (Shoerite Limited) is a Victorian shop and residence above, with a basement, constrained by the building's footprint, below. Except that even in this humble storage area there are two arches, one now brieze-blocked, that scooped out extra space by stretching under the carriage entrance of the once famous neighbouring inn, the King's Head. Decapitated brick columns show different periods of construction and that the shopfloor has been lowered (removing the entry step necessary in the days of earth and flint roads) at the basement's expense. In the cellar wall there are the remains of a small, blocked window that would once have given onto a skylight or grated airhole in the pavement. No trace of it now remains above and the brickwork is older than the smart Victorian stucco frontage would suggest. The same goes for the four steps up to an antique blocked doorway that must once have given onto the street, from where both entrances to the space below have been firmly erased from view. Only on the surface, though: what lies beneath reveals that what lies above is more ancient than its façade suggests.

Its neighbour is even more interesting. Just the other side of the narrow drive into the old innyard is No.5 High Street (Dorking Alterations). This houses an entrance into the ancient hostelry's cellars. Or one of them.

The King's Head was an early and leading inn, dating back to the late 17th century (and even before that as the Lower Chequers tavern; the rival Chequers Inn was across the road), and was for many years a leading transit point for anyone wishing

Right: Numbers 5 and 13 straddle the entrance to the old King's Head Inn's yard. Far right: Number 13, Shoerite: one of two arched cellar sections directly below the King's Head's carriage entrance.

Below: The cellar below No.5, part of the old King's Head. To the left of the stairs is a large arch and a truncated passage. The wooden flooring conceals a further cellar.

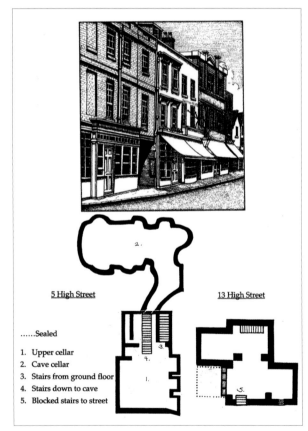

5 High Street   **13 High Street**

......Sealed

1. Upper cellar
2. Cave cellar
3. Stairs from ground floor
4. Stairs down to cave
5. Blocked stairs to street

to travel by stage to London. Charles Dickens cited it as the model for the *Pickwick Papers'* Marquis of Granby, while Sam Weller's father was probably modelled on the coachman of the Bull's Head, almost opposite. This is how Dickens described it: 'The bar window displayed a choice collection of geranium plants, and a well-dusted row of spirit phials. The open shutters bore a variety of golden inscriptions, eulogistic of good beds and neat wines; and the choice group of countrymen and hostlers lounging about the stable-door and horse-trough, afforded presumptive proof of the excellent quality of the ale and spirits which were sold within. Sam Weller paused, when he dismounted from the coach, to note all these little indications of a thriving business, with the eye of an experienced traveller; and having done so, stepped in at once, highly satisfied with everything he had observed.'

The author of the 1855 *A Hand-Book of Dorking* wrote that 'The accommodations of this vast establishment were once on the completest scale; and at that period it was noted for serving up water-sousey, a delicate fish, in great repute among the bon-vivant'. Later, despite the building of a large entertainment hall, 'it declined and the premises were let off and converted into shops and partly occupied by poor families'.

In his 1909 book *Highways and Byways in Surrey*, Eric Parker, whose pleasingly lyrical turn of phrase compensates for the sometimes questionable historical accuracy, wrote: 'You may still gaze at its unhappy walls and windows. The old lattices are boarded up, smashed with stones; the rooms are empty. When the post office came to stand at the corner, the King's Head became a tenement house; afterwards a ruin.'

The inn retrenched. It had straddled two important roads. Now parts were sold off, in particular its sizeable presence on the High Street. Then the bustling courtyard, vital for the stagecoach trade and long a venue for visiting players, went. The part of the building facing onto narrow little North Street remained virtually unaltered, much of it surviving as an inn into the 20th century.

In time the ex-premises on the High Street were remodelled and acquired an early Victorian façade. They got a second one, with Dutch gables, towards the end of that century. The old courtyard and North Street frontage (which faced, just feet away, yet another competitor, the Gun Inn) have all now been charmingly preserved as a café and small shops.

Entered, like its neighbour at No.13, through a hatch in the shop floor, the cellar at No.5 is a fine one, which reveals its evolution through different eras of brickwork, arches and some surviving antique beams. Typically, it has four substantial alcoves built into the walls for holding bottles. An intriguing short, narrow little corridor stub leads off on one side, complete with a niche that might have held a lamp and a curving roof that suggests how the space has changed over the years, and that more of it may have been filled or sealed off behind the existing walls during the generations of changes. Unusually, it is completely lined with brick, including the floor, except where that floor is made of timber panels. This arrangement seems quite normal until you notice gaps at the edges. Explore these, lie down, squeeze a camera in and you discover that there is a whole flight of steps leading into an intriguingly dark sand cave below.

Original timbers from the days of the old inn.

With the kind permission of the owner, a return visit was made and two wooden panels lifted, to make it possible to squeeze through. Entering the second chamber was one of those just-when-you-think-you've-seen-everything moments. Instead of the small square room suggested by rumours of a cell somewhere beneath the old pub, there is a cavernous historic chamber, with bays, alcoves and buttresses hacked into its sides. All overlooked by two carved skulls – placed above candelholding niches for maximum spectral effect – which must have been intended to frighten staff who made the journey into the darkness here, two storeys below the ground.

Gouged, deeply-shadowed cavities and shelves offer storage space for countless bottles and barrels, a neatly made square niche may have held a lamp. One large bay has an antique brick-strengthened arch roof and a possible blocked chute from the cellar above. In a corner a sand bunker holds a few lumps of coal, broken 20th century shop glass, empty canisters of Ilford and Kodak film and fragments of 19th century medicine bottles.

Inevitably, some of the graffiti, including two clumsily faked '1660's and a '1520', is by the boys who like to say 'F**k' (in this case Kev and Rick). Their work is

Below left: A way opened through the false floor to the chamber below the cellar
Below: Revealing this fine old staircase going two storeys below street level.

outnumbered by more of the beautiful, aged and authentic copybook script of past centuries: I Benwicke 177?, AL 1780, J Lynn 1817, Geo S Brown Aug 17 1859, H Ashworth, J Williams July 1888.

The sheer size of this cellar, larger even than the one above it, testifies to the popularity of the King's Head inn in its heyday. It is a breathtaking survivor and it's not the only one.

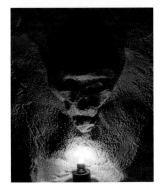

Above left: The unexpectedly large second cellar below the King's Head, now Dorking Alterations.
Above right: The size of the cellars reveals how booming the inn above must once have been. On the end wall is one of two carved skulls.
Right: Carved skulls designed to be spookily underlit by the candles that once illuminated the cavern – and to scare those who had to descend in search of supplies.

Below: Bay with brick-strengthened roof and possible blocked chute down.
Below right: Electrical fitting and remains of old medicine bottles from the shop's time as a chemist. It has also been a printers and a photographic shop.

At No.1 High Street, (now a café) a further shop was installed in the old King's Head. This became the site of Dorking's post office, a 19th century town landmark, despite the then deteriorating state of the increasingly subdivided old inn buildings. Access to its cellar has not been possible but from the tenant's description it has been lined and rationalised and no longer has the pleasing jigsaw puzzle character of the upper cellar at No.5.

The underground story of the King's Head doesn't end there. Just as on the surface the old inn was divided, walled off and altered, so too were its below ground spaces, creating a warren of three cellars. Around the corner, in narrow little North Street, the once grand tavern clung on to life and its licence until 1903, by which time it was a fraction of its original size, a tramps' lodging house with a lawless clientele and a drunken landlord. It is below this part that a third cellar (or fourth if you count the second deep level one at No.5) survives, its presence revealed by a fine pavement light outside. According to the shopowner the space below is wood-lined, eccentrically shaped and still has a blind staircase that would once have exited into the courtyard.

On North Street, the King's Head had a direct competitor: the Gun Inn, directly opposite and almost touching distance away. A further pub, the once huge Queen's Arms, of which it had at one time formed a part, was literally next door (now a bank).

The Gun, at No.1 North Street, was housed in a fine 16th century building which thankfully was saved from planned demolition in the 1970s. The trapdoor to its cellar has recently been floored over, making access difficult, but the space below what is now the Bourneside Gallery is described as being square, brick-lined, and with the old wooden beams that support the ground floor ceiling continuing into the basement, where they are supported on brick plinths.

Pavement lights, like this one to the North Street basement of the King's Head, are a common but little noticed feature of the town's walkways – and an indicator of a cellar below.

The road surface (not including pavements) between the two competing pubs is just over seven feet across. Just wide enough for the panzers massing across the channel in 1940, when sockets were dug in the tarmac between both inns, into which girders would be dropped to make a tank trap; a desperate last ambush point to stop the enemy invasion force making it to the High Street and the road to London. It is genuinely sobering to stand and realise that from these two pub buildings, soldiers and Home Guardsmen would have swarmed out, armed with molotov cocktails and sticky bombs, in a desperate, do or die attempt to halt an armoured column at this narrowest of pinchpoints.

The weakest stone thrower could once have hit five taverns from the King's Head's doorway. One was the White Lion (now the St Catherine's Hospice Shop) at 8-10 South Street. It is uncertain whether this fine little 17th century building was built as an inn, or was, like many others, converted from a dwelling. The original basement, now divided into two, appears too small for pub use, a shortcoming that seems to have been solved by buying the neighbouring building, No.12 (now The Edit), and driving a passage through into its cellar. This would have offered the additional advantage of an entrance direct into the shared inn yard and stable area behind both buildings.

Charles Rose described the White Lion as being 'besieged' on Saturday nights by workers from the chalk pits eager 'to attend that welcome spot – the pay table'. (In 1842 payment to coal miners and colliery workers in pubs was prohibited by law, condemned as an encouragement to drunkenness and the loss of a week's wages in a single night.) This otherwise blameless (if you set aside the rather odd presence of peepholes in its bedroom doors) little inn was closed by the licensing authorities

*Far left: The former King's Head (left) and Gun (right), still with the bracket that held its inn sign, are practically within touching distance. The Queen's Arms was next door to the latter.
Left: Lions' heads – carved by someone who has never seen one – decorate a window at the old Gun.*

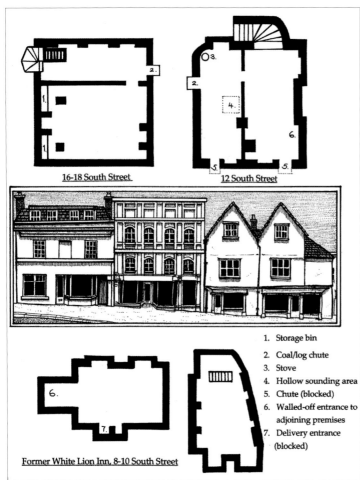

1. Storage bin
2. Coal/log chute
3. Stove
4. Hollow sounding area
5. Chute (blocked)
6. Walled-off entrance to adjoining premises
7. Delivery entrance (blocked)

in Edwardian times as surplus to the town's requirements, then divided into two shops. Its cellar was likewise split into two, both now part-filled with earth, and the way through to No.12's basement sealed off. Over the years, the former pub has hosted various concerns: a cobblers, dyers and cleaners, clothes shops, and a tailors. Owner Ian Cameron, co-author of both buildings' award-winning 1990s restoration, reports finding a wealth of lost cotton reels, wooden soldiers and thimbles beneath the floorboards. Meanwhile, No.12 was, from 1893 to 1958, a tobacconist and confectioners named Boorers and, later, Ye Old Oake Shop.

There is a lovely description of the premises

Above right: The former White Lion and its neighbour, whose cellar it took over.

as it was in 1920, written by one of the family, Elizabeth Green, née Boorer: 'The shop was small and dark. You went down two steps to go in and from the door the floor sloped away unevenly, down towards the counter at the back. Coming in from the sunlit street, you felt you were entering a cave. Perfumes met you as you went in, snuff, cigars, tobacco, chocolate and, over all, a certain stale mustiness. The ceiling was beamed with old ship's timbers and the whole place was very old. A warm greeting from my aunt and uncle; the counter flap lifted up and I would be in the Holy of Holies, behind. In the entrance door there was a small counter inserted and arrayed under it were boxes of all kinds of sweet things. I remember locust beans – hard and brown and sweet, probably somewhat dusty, too – chocolate drops, aniseed balls, sherbet and black licorice, not yet surrounded with colour … a halfpenny bought a feast.'

Right: The conserved (thanks to the enthusiasm of its owner), part-filled, left hand cellar of the old White Lion, showing at the far end the passage built to connect with Number 12 next door. Far right: Storage bays and the trap down from the shop, once an inn, above.

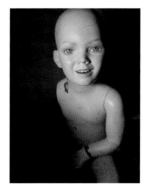

Number 12's cellar, with its old coal stove preserved in situ, remains in use, part shopfloor, part storeroom. Like many in the town, the chute or trapdoor entrances down from the street have been paved over without trace but a fine coal hole cover, a ringed square slab of stone far from the elegant cast iron examples of the later Victorian era, lives on in the alley above.

Ian Cameron described the urgency of flooring this cellar as part of the restoration. At some point, its original sandstone floor had been given a thin screed, probably to allow better storage for the tobacconists' goods. He said that he will always regret the need to concrete over an intriguingly hollow-sounding patch that may have covered a further cave, or possibly a well, below.

Next door, the left hand side of the divided pub cellar lives on in earthy darkness; living history unsuspected beneath the customers' feet. Blackened and heavily cobwebbed, the right hand half is a kind of museum to shop use, heaped with the jetsam of recent decades. Mounds of plastic clothes hangers crackle underfoot. A child mannequin remains forever young next to a discarded 1980s cash register. Nearby, among the detritus of old fittings, another register is slowly sinking into the soil.

The tides of time flow over our surroundings, covering them or washing them away but sometimes unearthing them too. Just next to No.12 and the former White Lion, is the early 19th century Nos.16-18. Originally a private residence, it later housed a grocery and provision merchant licensed to sell alcohol. A recent renovation there removed the previous fittings and modern flooring to reveal fine old floorboards and a pub-like double hatch. Once it would have led to a roomy brick- and stone-lined cellar which can now be entered from behind the shop. Inside the original alcoves live on, alongside large brick storage bins very similar to those at the White Horse. In the alleyway above another hand-carved ringed stone slab covers the coal chute that once fed into the cellar.

Another in its time much-missed hostelry was The Bell Hotel at 57 West Street. Its

Abovel left: The impressively cobwebbed right hand cellar below the old White Lion.
Above middle: A face in the darkness below the old White Lion, now a charity shop.
Above: The cellar charts the premises' long history as various shops following the inn's closure.

Far left: The cellars at Number 12, with characteristic alcove in far wall, once belonged to the neighbouring White Lion pub.
Left: Stairs up.

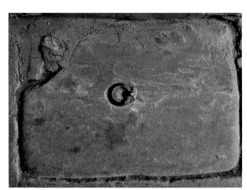

Above: 16-18 South Street.
Above middle: Fourth in a row of cellars, those at 16-18 South Street. The far wall is given over to storage bays.
Above right: Coal/log chute from above. A similar hand-carved, ringed stone cover also serves number 12 next door.

closure in the 1980s put an end to almost four centuries of innkeeping and brewing on the site, although thankfully leaving the listed 18th century premises intact (now occupied by Acquis Limited). Below ground is a neat, bricklined two-room cellar, now used for document storage. One half has been given a modern cement floor. Behind the shelving there are a few arched alcoves for bottle storage. A larger arch, next to the chimney for an original stove which would have sat on a brick dais, has been filled. It may have housed a coal chute or even a coal bunker. The barrel hatch down from the street or the inn's carriage entrance has been paved over.

The design of the cellars is efficient and businesslike. They would have served the business above well. According to customer accounts, this was a happy hostelry. To the end, it had faithful visitors who liked to return to its quaint (but probably not terribly profitable) rooms and the narrow staircase that led to them.

The second section of the cellar retains a particularly fine stone-flagged floor. Interestingly, the thick wall between the two rooms conceals a rubble-filled void. It appears this hollow wall was made extra wide to provide better support for the floors above. The removal of old joists has exposed a peephole into the space inside, into which in the 1970s some empty ginger ale bottles were popped.

Tollgates, where wheeled traffic stopped to pay dues that went towards the upkeep of main roads, proved a powerful magnet for the siting of inns to serve passersby and the carriage trade. One of these was the Beehive on London Road, close to the Stepping Stones. Beamed and inglenooked, it served as an inn from 1755 until 1887 when, with the Georgian house next door, it was converted into a handsome residence. It still is, with a picturesque garden that belies its tactical location, which in wartime meant the Dorking anti-tank ditch ran alongside the lawn and down to the Mole, closely protected by a now-removed pillbox on the A24 outside. Its large pub cellars have been incorporated into the house's living space, enhanced by the preservation of features such as the original beams, stone walls and supporting arch.

Below: The former Bell Inn, now home to Acquis Limited.
Below middle: The second section of the Bell's cellar, showing the surviving, nicely stone-flagged floor.
Below right: The old inn's carriageway entrance. Immediately opposite is the ex-Rose and Crown pub.

Thanks to *Time Gentlemen Please* we know that the George Inn, a tavern that operated from the 1500s until 1818, was located at No.47 High Street (now the Lemon Tree gift shop). The frontage is deceptive: another case of a 1800s façade concealing something much older behind. The view from historic little Cape Passage reveals an antique rear and roofline. The shop's sidewall, in full public view in the passage arch, predates even this, and may stretch to as far back as 1500. It was constructed from blocks of stone with wooden beam support, all now covered with half a millennium's worth of paint. Unusually, this construction continues right down into the original cellar. In the pub's three-century history, a large number of alcoves and bottle bays in stone and handmade brick were added, but the original, rock-like

Above left: View from the stableyard of the old pub, looking towards the entrance from West Street.
Above: On the building's front, the posts supporting the first floor are decorated with carved reminders of the inn's name.

Far left: Lemon Tree and Amplifon and the higher, smaller cellar at No.47.

building stones can be seen in the street-facing cellar wall and, unpainted and original as the Tudor mason left them, from inside one of the bays. An arched alcove, sealed at its top, may have housed a barrel ramp or a coal and wood hatch; it is also possible that there was barrel access from the back yard and stable area that was closed off and bricked over after the pub closed.

The large, bayed cellar is approached from a branching stairway, that continues to a slightly smaller cellar, which is lower-ceilinged and less deep than the main one. The brickwork in this appears to be 19th century and it may be either an old space that was later brick-lined or an extension made after the building changed to retail use (and from the 1840s as a branch of the London and County Bank). The premises appear frequently in Victorian and Edwardian photos as the home of the London Boot Company, heavily bedecked with its wares and painted advertisements ('Stop and Study. Tip Top Value In Up To Date Foot Wear'). Its gaslit Victorian modernity concealed the fact that below the ground and behind the façade, the structures of the Tudor era lived on.

The joined building next door (Nos.41-45) probably has a similarly historic basement, given its original occupation by a private bank and then later by Maybank's, another of the

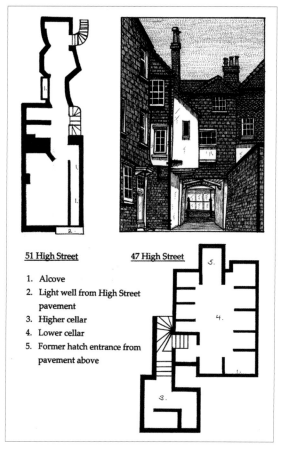

51 High Street   **47 High Street**

1. Alcove
2. Light well from High Street pavement
3. Higher cellar
4. Lower cellar
5. Former hatch entrance from pavement above

Right: Facing south in the lower, main cellar, first dug in Tudor times

Below: Facing north. The whole cellar is lined with bottle and barrel storage bays in brick and stone.
Below middle: Climb inside one of the bottle bays and part of the original stone cellar wall is visible, unpainted for 500 years.
Below right: A blocked entrance to the roadway is flanked by original stone walls.

town's big 19th century wine and spirit merchants. Unfortunately entry has not been possible to this cellar, which is enticingly described as 'big, dark and spooky'.

On the other side of the old George, just across Cape Passage, is No.51 High Street (Amplifon), which dates back to the 18th century. Recollecting the 1870s and 80s, William Dinnage identified the building as being the premises of John Chart, a cabinet maker and upholsterer who also did business as an undertaker, specialising in burying the town's poorest and most wretched residents. Dinnage wrote: 'I think he was successful in obtaining the contracts for the burial of the workhouse paupers from the Board of Guardians of the Poor. The pauper corpses were conveyed to the Dorking Cemetery in a two-wheeled hearse drawn by one horse. Every economy had to be considered and there was a great saving of unnecessary furniture and embellishments of which

Right: Pavement light at 51 High Street, seen from below.
Far right: The space on the right would have held a large sink.

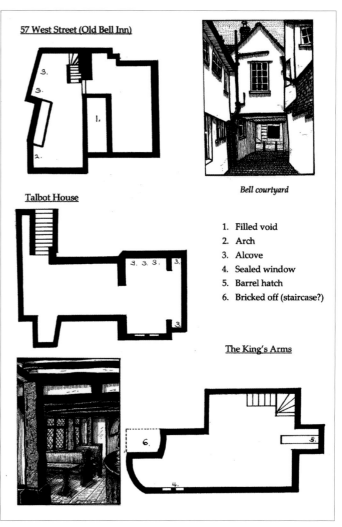

57 West Street (Old Bell Inn)

Talbot House

Bell courtyard

1. Filled void
2. Arch
3. Alcove
4. Sealed window
5. Barrel hatch
6. Bricked off (staircase?)

The King's Arms

the successful undertakers were fully aware. They carried out the melancholy work accordingly.'

The cellar is roomy enough to have served all three trades. It stretches the length of the building, from front, where it is part lit by an attractive pastel-glassed pavement light that can be seen from the street above, to back. It is reached by two staircases, one from just behind the shop and one at the back, leading straight down to a scullery area, where there was once an almost bath-sized sink. That must have been useful in at least one of John Chart's trades.

One of the pleasures of the underworld, along with its atmospheric darkness and habit of enveloping and preserving the past in its damp embrace, is the mysteries it presents. When historic buildings are studied and listed, the one part that often escapes analysis is that beneath the earth. Into this void rumours of secret passages, lost boats, ghosts, Roman murals, whores' tunnels and secret churches are gleefully shovelled. To achieve any kind of reliable explanation and origin for Dorking's underground spaces, the physical evidence has to be combined with any surviving historical data. It's basic detective work. It's part of what makes it interesting.

The jigsaw pieces are there at Dorking's oldest pub, the King's Arms on West Street. This fine old one-time coaching inn was created in the 17th or 18th century from three timber-framed, wattle and daub farm cottages dating back in part to the early 15th century. One of the pleasures of visiting today is to notice the different floor levels, cubby holes, fireplaces and massive beams of three ancient houses combined into one richly wood-panelled and historic pub.

The cellar is entered from a door behind the bar, down an unexpectedly low and very narrow staircase. It isn't huge and certainly isn't high ceilinged. Unusually, the barrel hatch lies towards the rear of the building, rather than out front. One end holds a very old blocked and wood-beamed window, very similar to one at Talbot House, and an unexplained curved wall whose promise of going somewhere is immediately terminated by blocking brickwork that is pitch-painted to resist dampness. A bulging wall next to the opening finishes the job of sealing off something. The rumour that goes with it is that it's another tunnel to a brothel.

Top left: The King's Arms, Dorking's oldest surviving inn.

Right: Hatch down to the King's Arms cellar, which only entered service as a beer store two decades ago. Far right: Before then the cellar's history is likely to have stretched back to the original 15th century cottages that later became the inn. Note the beams and stone walls.

A better solution is suggested by the shape and features of the cellars, plus the information that the main barrel room was in a surface outhouse until twenty years ago, and old records that describe a ground floor tap room and wood and coal (but not beer) cellars. The current main cellar is likely to date right back to its antique forerunners, the farm cottages. The answer to the irregularities and the walled offshoot is that these were two unjoined, single cellars of widely differing sizes, probably dug when those original early houses were built. Then, centuries later, the cellars were knocked together when three became one. There may even be a chance that the third house also had one that was considered superfluous and covered over. The mysterious curved wall is likely to be, not a tunnel, but the remains of a destroyed staircase up to the middle cottage that would once have emerged where the pub's gents' toilets are now. A short section of stairs may even survive behind that centuries old end wall.

The subterranean history of the town frequently throws up whole networks of unsuspected and coincidental links. Names appear and reappear. Brewers become wine merchants become cave owners; shops open, close, are taken over by figures familiar for the underground traces they've left elsewhere. Authors, business owners, professionals and the gentry leave a name, an advert, a bill of sale here, own a shop with fine cellars there, and are met with on memorials, parish records or when, on hands and knees, you literally stumble over their tombs underground.

The pub basement was originally the cellars of two houses – a third may still be down there, bricked off.

So, it's not a surprise that the cellared King's Arms is associated with another riotous subterranean episode from Dorking's history of dissent (or vandalism). In his 1724 *A Tour thro' the Whole Island of Great Britain*, Daniel Defoe recorded that in the shade of a great beech tree on the summit of Box Hill a 'little vault or cave' – possibly a natural cavern in the chalk – was being used as a meeting point for coachloads of gentlemen and ladies fresh from the fashionable spa and louche pleasure gardens of Epsom and hellbent on 'diversion or debauchery, or perhaps both'.

Defoe explained: 'A vintner

who kept the King's-Arms-Inn, at Darking, taking notice of the constant and unusual flux of company thither, took the hint from the prospect of his advantage, which offer'd, and obtaining leave of Sir Adam Brown, whose mannor and land it was, furnish'd this little cellar or vault with tables, chairs, &c. and with wine and eatables to entertain the ladies and gentlemen on Sunday nights, as above; and this was so agreeable to them as that it encreased the company exceedingly … the place was like a little fair; so that at length the country began to take notice of it, and it was very offensive, especially to the best governed

What at first sight looks like a passage going nowhere is revealed as a blocked-off staircase going up to the middle of the three cottages that now make up the ancient inn.

people; this lasted some years, I think two or three, and tho' complaint was made of it to Sir Adam Brown, and the neighbouring justices; alledging the revelling, and the indecent mirth that was among them, and on the Sabbath Day too, yet it did not obtain a suitable redress: whereupon a certain set of young men, of the town of Darking, and perhaps prompted by some others, resenting the thing also, made an unwelcome visit to the place once on a Saturday night, just before the usual time of their wicked mirth, and behold when the coaches and ladies, &c. from Epsome appear'd the next afternoon, they found the cellar or vault, and all that was in it, blown up with gun-powder … That action put an end to their revels for a great while; nor was the place ever repaired that I heard of, at least it was not put to the same wicked use that it was employ'd in before.'

As proven by his brilliant historical novel *A Journal of the Plague Year* (whose narrator's brother flees from London to Dorking in the hope of escaping the disease), Defoe was an expert at fictionalising true events. We cannot now know whether there is any exaggeration in his story of pranksters blowing an underground drinking den to pieces and escaping unpunished. You may still hear stories of hidden chalk caves on the hill, but never with a findable location attached. The site of Defoe's great beech on the very top of Box Hill is long since lost to memory. As late as the 1980s, there was an interesting depression in the ground next to the road near the viewpoint in which fragments of old bottles could be seen, but they were from the 19th century. They might just reflect the filling in, by a later generation, of the ruins left by what would have been the most dangerous, daring and explosive prank ever committed by the town's endlessly recurring naughty boys.

Please **DO NOT** park in this alley. There is no vehicular access. You will cause further collapse of the drains and possibly the cellar.

CHAPTER TWELVE

Hidden depths

Despite Dorking's superabundance of pubs and caves, its beery cockfighting and cheery riots, exhibitionists and eccentrics, alleged witches and highwaymen, and its stories of underground sects and subterranean sex, tunnellers and tarts, it still somehow failed to make it into the county rhyme:

'Sutton for mutton,
Carshalton for beeves,
Epsom for whores,
and Ewell for thieves.'

By living even a few generations we become time travellers, suddenly wondering when we stopped answering telephones by stating their number or when shopkeepers ceased counting out change into your hand. We remember the past but evolve in a succession of presents. Subterranean structures, made redundant by refrigeration and regulations on food and drink storage, then closed off as too dark or dank or dangerous, don't.

The town's hand-dug, often crudely made, sometimes dripping cellars are perfect time capsules. Unchanged, they take us back to a Dorking of Swing Riots and arson by starving farmworkers, of invasion scares, yeomanries and militias, disease, poverty and public execution, and of dread of a poorhouse that was so large that when it was converted for a 20th century hospital, two thirds of it was demolished. Yet when the area was also a ferment of the arts, an inspiration for artists and authors, and all overlooked from a scenic distance by the mansions of men comfortable with the idea of housing tortoises in luxury while workers went homeless, or spending the equivalent of 750 years of a farm labourer's annual wage on the fraternal gift of a garden extension.

Over the years, many major subterranean structures have been destroyed, many of them shockingly recently. Those losses continue. Nevertheless, enough remains below the town to reward years of study, whether lost but not forgotten or forgotten but not lost.

Prime in the first category must be the town's once nationally-important lime industry, carried on in the huge and now filled-in workings within the town, as well as at Betchworth. From the 1980s to the 2000s the chalkpits there lost their once vast cliff to landfill. Since then many buildings have collapsed or been demolished. It is disturbing how much has disappeared in recent years, and how little remains of the grade II listed kilns that were scheduled under the Ancient Monuments and Archaeological Areas Act in 2004, despite them being described as unique, exceptionally well preserved and an important local amenity and educational resource. So go and see them soon, using appropriate care if approaching closely.

A number of buildings remain, at least for now, while some of the destroyed ones were captured in the 1970 film *Scream and Scream Again*, which used the quarry's other-worldly scale and everywhere-white-coated scenery to considerable effect. The same is true of its neighbouring quarry's appearances in the 1976 *Doctor Who* series *The Deadly Assassin* (the quarries made such regular appearances in episodes of the classic era series that they virtually count as one of the Doctor's assistants). Low budget 1967 Brit sci-fi *The Terrornauts* utilised the location to less striking effect but a vivid reminder of just how huge and monumental the landmark quarry face used to be can be found in a superb TV clip filmed by Lew Grade's ITC company in 1965. Shot for an episode of *The Baron*, it shows, with the help of a costly sacrificial automatic camera, a white Jaguar plummeting to its destruction. (You can find it on YouTube by looking for 'ITC white jag'). The footage was so good that it was reused in eight more of the company's productions, including *The Saint*, *Randall & Hopkirk Deceased*, *Jason King* and *Hammer House of Mystery and Suspense*. (They are all lovingly recorded at www.randallandhopkirk.org.uk/features_white_jag.htm). A red Renault filmed flying off the cliff made almost as many appearances, including in *Father Ted*. To save money this one didn't have a camera in it, so its appearance is usually preceded with an insert of the shot from inside the Jag (the white bonnet is the giveaway).

Lost, like the Dorking town limeworks and Betchworth's cliff, is *Lloyd of the C.I.D*, a 1932 cinema serial filmed at Deepdene House that is currently on the British Film Institute's list of most wanted missing British films. It charted the attempts by international criminal and master of disguise The Panther to steal a sacred Egyptian amulet owned by Lord Hale of 'Deep-dene Manor' and the efforts of Chief Inspector Lloyd to thwart him and rival amulet thieves (the priests of the Temple of Amenhotep). Some of the chapter titles give a flavour of the action: *The Green Spot Murder*, *The Panther Strikes*, *Tracked by Wireless*, *The Death Ray*, *Imprisoned in the North Tower*.

The film's slightly desperate US advance publicity is a mine of cheesy invention. Apparently, its lead actor had been considered 'a little white god by the Australian bushmen by whom he had been captured', aged five. Meanwhile, every 'venerable British manor has a ghost', and actress Emily Fitzroy, who played Deepdene's spectre, 'had a most unpleasant experience'. While reportedly still in full ghost makeup one night she was 'horrified to see two strange men quietly enter the room. The intruders, on seeing what they imagined to be a replica of death itself, clutched each other by the arms and beat a hasty retreat. The two strangers were visitors and had mistaken Miss Fitzroy's bedroom for the bathroom' (probably not the first time that excuse had been heard at the hotel). Deepdene House was described as having nearly 100 rooms, 37 chambers and vaulted cellars, and being 'situated in a beautiful four-hundred acre park in the town of Dorking. From its towers and age-old groves one can look out on the picturesque but barren Sussex moors.'

Although very few people seem to have seen it, the twelve-part serial was shown in ITV's HTV region in 1977, so there may be some hope of a print being found. Shot at the nadir of Deepdene's fortunes and with a strong whiff of Maundy Gregory-ish desperation for additional cashflow, it would certainly be interesting to view.

There is a heartbreakingly long list of lost or sealed sites not previously mentioned in this book: the now incredibly rare Tett Turret mini-revolving sunken pillbox that guarded the drive to Denbies, Cotmandene Cottage's 'garden grotto and cabinet collection of curiosities' mentioned in *A Picturesque Promenade*, at least two venerable cellars destroyed in the building of the original Waitrose in South Street, the once highly modern staff shelter now resting beneath the croquet lawn of Milton Court (built when the mansion served as the wartime headquarters of Henley Cables) or the caves reported in the *Surrey Mirror* in 1889 under the headline 'Singular Discovery at Dorking'. This told how workmen laying the town's new sewers 'were engaged at the shop of Messrs. Kendall and Sons, High-street, and in the course of opening up the earth came upon some brick work. This was broken through, and some of the bricks fell with a hollow thud. Thereupon Mr. A.G. Brandram crawled through the aperture, and finding there was a deep cave-like room beneath, lowered a ladder and descended to a depth of about 15 feet. He found himself in a cave some dozen feet square, cut out in the sand-rock, and was somewhat startled to discover in the centre of the floor a yawning chasm. This proved to be the mouth of a well, over 30 feet deep. A peculiarity of the well is that it is quite square. Leading out of the cave was a doorway, and passing through this the explorer found himself in a room of larger size, beautifully formed. On the walls were cut the names of "Caffyn," with the date of 1808, and another dated 1818.' Pleasingly, 'the discovery of these caves caused some excitement, and they were inspected by a number of people'. The shop, like its neighbour the Red Lion, was later demolished and replaced with a bland arcade.

A member of the Surrey Antique Bottle Collectors' Club owns three Bellarmine jugs (16th or 17th century pottery flagons), bought still wrapped in pages from a 1950s *Dorking Advertiser*. That was when the seller, a builder, had been working at No.99 High Street, and come upon a 'cellar full of them'. Mildly interested, he picked up the specimens that he would sell years later. Now worth not too far off £500 each, there should be scores or maybe hundreds more still down there. With a Barclays Bank built on top.

It's a sad litany of loss. However, some, at least, of Dorking's once incredible underground heritage remains. Undoubtedly, more remains forgotten and sealed, traceable through records and observation, though it now appears likely that, unless there is a significant change in attitude, the future of most of those sites is to be destroyed and built over. In addition, a quarter of the premises approached for this book either refused access or ignored all requests, adding over twenty more caves and cellars to the total of known historical sites.

In Dorking, as in many towns, it is worth walking with your gaze high and directed across the road. Hand-carved beams frame doors and windows, green men gaze with malice from column tops, terracotta flowers bloom, a dragon flexes its wings, lions bare their teeth, on the old candle factory a brick owl ponders the message 'Let There Be Light', and behind Georgian and Victorian parapets earlier rooflines weave and sag. But break the rule, tread the same streets and keep your head down, and something else is revealed: a wonderland of ways down, a montage of manholes, an invitation of entrances. Building after building, shop after shop, with a disused hatch, a leaf-choked grating, a never-lifted coalhole cover or railinged steps down to a long-locked door. Ventilators, manhole covers, filled and grilled cellar entrances. More places than you could ever get permission to prise open and visit.

There's a whole town down there.

Where to visit

The surface interiors and exteriors of the retail establishments, hostelries and places of worship described in this book can be enjoyed while visiting them or shopping. Several serve refreshments. The following are also open for visits:

South Street Caves: **www.dorkingmuseum.org.uk/south-street-caves**

Deepdene Trail: **www.deepdenetrail.co.uk**

Dorking Museum: **www.dorkingmuseum.org.uk**

Betchworth Castle: visitable by following the fingerposted route through the five bar gate from the old road, just off the A25 by the sign to Betchworth Park Golf Club. There are railings around those parts that require particular care. The castle is regularly opened during Heritage Open Days.

Betchworth Chalkpits: **www.surreywildlifetrust.org/reserves/betchworth-quarry-lime-kilns**

Brockham Limeworks: **www.surreywildlifetrust.org/reserves/brockham-limeworks**

The Castle Mill (RH4 1NN) caves can be viewed from the adjoining public footpath, which runs down the west side of the Watermill Pub car park.

Part of the White Hart cellars can be seen through a grille in the pub's backyard smoking area, which is usually open until 9 pm.

The Nower trenches can be found by following the westerly footpath from Bracken Lodge, which is near to the car park off the A25. You will immediately start passing the sites of former Nissen huts; the banks on either side of you are partly made with their remains. Just before you reach the footpath's end and the A25 take the blue arrow-marked bridlepath on the left. When it forks take the right hand way, passing an old water tank on your left, then keep an eye out for the practice wall and trenches.

Box Hill WW2 defences: **www.pillbox-study-group.org.uk/war-walks/dorking-ghq-line**
The mobilisation centre is next to the National Trust tearooms and car park. It can be visited at any time, but not entered.

Reigate Caves: **www.reigatecaves.com**

River Mole swallow holes: **www.mvgs.org.uk/MVGS%20Files/Walks/Mole%20Gap%20pamplet.pdf**

Westcott air raid shelter and engine collection: regularly opened during Heritage Open Days.

Acknowledgements

My thanks to all those who have assisted, whether by permitting access or helping with information, including all the institutions and establishments mentioned in the text, as well as: Rosie Adams; Kathy Atherton; Ruth Azzopardi; Alex Bagnall; Ross Baker; David J Blow; Colin Brewer; Graeme Bridger; Frank Bruce; Peter Bunn; Peter Burgess; Paul Butcher; Nikki Bynum; Ian Cameron; Peter Camp; Elaine Davis; Dorking cave guides past and present; Andrew Dorman; Dorking Local History Group; Dorking Museum; Simon Dykes; Michael Fleming; Mark Griffiths, Lauren Francis; Sue Hales; Susannah Horne; Michael Hammett; Nick Hands-Clarke; Celia and Anthony Harcombe; Nick Harman; Dan Heymann; Martin Higgins; Preet Hislop; Peter Hollands; Sue Jamieson; Natasha Jones; Jana Kašparová; Sarah Keech; Iain Laurenson; Stephen Law; Pam Lintott; Patti Lister; Simon Mallalieu; Gurdeep Manku; Lisa Martin; Alistair McLean; members of Subterranea Britannia; Andrew Mitchell; Mole Valley District Council press office; James Morgan; George Morjaria; Dave Morley; Ryan Neal; Jean Neve; Penny Newsom; Peter Nimmo; Peter Olejnik; Lu Meng Pam; Ketan Patel; Jim Paulett; Clive Penfold; Claire Pickett; Joel Pyke; Mark Rogers; Bobbie Rounthwaite; Richard Selley; Paul Sowan; staff of the De Vere Wotton House Hotel; staff of Robert Dyas; Georgina Stone; staff of Talbot House Antiques Centre; Sarah Thomas; Sue Tombs; Mark Wakeford; Colin Waters; Lynn Whitfield; Scott Wilkie; Helen Wilson.

References

Alexander, M. (1985). *Tales of Old Surrey*. Newbury: Countryside Books.

Alexander, M. (2004). *A Surrey Garland*. Newbury: Countryside Books.

Allen, T. (1831). *A History of the County of Surrey*. London: Isaac Taylor Hinton.

Anon (believed to be Dennis, J.). (1855). *A Hand-Book of Dorking*. Dorking: J. Rowe Reprinted (1974). Dorking: Kohler and Coombes.

Atherton, K. (2015). *Dorking in the Great War*. Barnsley: Pen and Sword Military.

Attlee, J. *Reminiscences of Old Dorking*. (1912). Reprinted in Kohler, M.K. (1977). *Memories of Old Dorking*. Dorking: Kohler and Coombes.

Brayley, E. (1850). *A Topographical History of Surrey*. London: G. Willis.

Brandon, P. (1998). *A History of Surrey*. Chichester. Phillimore & Co. Ltd.

Bright, J.S. (1876). *Dorking, a History of the Town, with a Description of the Distinguished Residences, Remarkable Places, Walks and Drives, and Literary Associations*. Dorking: R.J. Clark.

Cook, A. (2008). *Cash for Honours*. Chalford: The History Press.

Defoe, D . (1724-1727). *A Tour Thro' the Whole Island of Great Britain, Divided into Circuits or Journeys*. First edition published in three volumes for J. Osborn, S. Birt, D. Browne, J. Hodges, A. Millar, J. Whiston, and J. Robinson.

Dinnage, W. (1963). *Recollections of Old Dorking*. Reprinted in Kohler, M.K. (1977). *Memories of Old Dorking*. Dorking: Kohler and Coombes.

Emmerson, A. and Beard, T. (2004). *London's Secret Tubes*. Harrow: Capital Transport.

Harding, K. (1997). *Dorking Revisited*. Stroud: Sutton Publishing Ltd.

Harper, C and Kershaw, J. (1923). *The Downs and The Sea: Wild Life and Scenery in Surrey, Sussex and Kent Illustrated by the Authors*. London: Cecil Palmer.

Henderson, J. and Hillman, B. and Pearman, H. (1968). *More Secret Tunnels in Surrey*. London: Chelsea Speleological Society.

Higgins, B. and Ettlinger, V. (2001). *The Great House on Butter Hill* in *Dorking History 2001*. Dorking: Dorking Local History Group.

Hole, C. (1941). *English Custom and Usage*. London: BT Batsford Ltd.

Jackson, A. (1989). *Around Dorking in Old Photographs*. Gloucester: Alan Sutton Publishing.

Jackson, A. (editor). (1991). *Dorking: A Surrey Market Town through Twenty Centuries*. Dorking: Dorking Local History Group.

Knight, D. (1989). *Dorking in Wartime*. Dorking: David Knight.

Langford, D. and Docking, J. (2017) *Time Gentlemen, Please: the Story of Dorking Pubs*. Dorking: Cockerel Press.

L'Estrange, E. (1929). *Witch Hunting and Witch Trials. The Indictments for Witchcraft from the Records of 1373 Assizes Held for the Home Circuit, A.D. 1559-1736*. New York: Routledge Library Press.

Mayhew, H. (1851). *London Labour and the London Poor*. London: George Woodfall and Son.

Mercer, D. and Jackson, A. (1996). *The Deepdene Dorking*. Dorking: Dorking Local History Group.

Pitkin, P. *A Walk in the Mole Gap: Terraces & Swallow Holes*. (2003). Dorking: Mole Valley Geological Society.

Moul, D. and Thompson, G. *Picturesque Surrey*. (1902). Reprinted (1985). Weybridge: Contour Books.

Molyneux, J. *Memories of World War II in Surrey*, in *Dorking History (2017)*. Dorking. Dorking Local History Group.

Parker, E. *Highways and Byways in Surrey*. (1909). London: MacMillan and Company.

Parker, E. *Surrey*. (1947). London: Robert Hale Limited.

Pearman, H. (compiler). (1963). *Secret Tunnels in Surrey*. Powys: Chelsea Speleological Society.

Pearman, H. (compiler). (1976). *Caves and Tunnels in South-East England*. London: Chelsea Speleological Society.
(1978). *Caves and Tunnels in South-East England Part 2*. London: Chelsea Speleological Society.

Rose, C. (1878). *Recollections of Old Dorking*. Guildford: West Surrey Times. Reprinted in Kohler, M.K. (1977). *Memories of Old Dorking*. Dorking: Kohler and Coombes.

Ruddy, J. (2003). *British Anti-Invasion Defences 1940-1945*. Storrington: Historic Military Press.

Smith, V. *Defence Against Invasion: Reigate Fort* in *Surrey Archaeological Collections*, Volume 98 (2014).

Sowan, P. *Planning and construction of Surrey County Council's five World War II deep tunnelled air-raid shelters and related subsurface schemes*, in *Subterranea*, issue 33, September 2013.

Sowan, P. *Joseph Peter, Lime-worker of Dorking* in S*urrey Archaeology Bulletin 391* (2006), pp7-8.

Sowan, P. *The Surrey hearthstone mining industry and the hearthstone trade*. Newsletter Surrey Industrial History Group 217 (2018), pp15-18.

Sowan, P. *Accidents at the Brockham Hearthstone Mine and Limeworks*, 1910-1934. Wealden Cave and Mine Society:
www.wcms.org.uk/cgi-bin/wcmsarchive.pl?archid=brockham_accidents_nov2004.

Timbs, J. (1822). *A Picturesque Promenade Round Dorking*. London: John Warren.

Wedgwood, A. (Ed). *A History of the Church and Parish of St. Martin's Dorking*. (1990). Dorking: Friends of St Martin's.

Weight, C. (1988). *The South Street Caves Dorking*. Dorking: Dorking Local History Group.

Index

5 Dene Street   141-143
62 Dene Street   115

1 High Street   146
5 High Street   143-146
13 High Street   143-144
18 High Street   91
20-28 High Street   92
32-38 High Street   87
37-39 High Street   133
40 High Street   91
41-45 High Street   151
47 High Street   151-152
51 High Street   151-153
54 High Street   90,92
56a High Street   91
62 High Street   87
66 High Street   87
70 High Street   87-88, 92
74 High Street   89
78 High Street   89-90, 92
81-85 High Street   57-60
82 High Street   89
94-98 High Street   87
99 High Street   159
100-102 High Street   87
104 High Street   87
123 High Street   138
125-129 High Street   139
136 High Street   86
150-154 High Street   115,117
155/157 High Street   118-119
156 High Street   115-117
159 High Street   117-118
176 High Street   139
220-222 High Street   142-143
277 High Street   115
294 High Street   55-57

1 North Street   147

2 South Street   71-72
4 South Street   72
8-10 South Street   147-149
12 South Street   147-149
16-18 South Street   148-149
39 South Street   80-81
77 South Street   119
81 South Street   81-82
97 South Street   74-75
98-100 South Street   75-79

8 West Street   55, 60
9-10 West Street   137
16 West Street   72, 74
17-18 West Street   72-74
19 West Street   72-73
24 West Street   140

36 West Street   140
45 West Street   153-155
51-52 West Street   138-139
53 West Street   137
55 West Street   137
57 West Street   149-150
58-61 West Street   100

11 Rose Hill   74

A
Act of Toleration   11, 99
Acquis Limited   150
Alexander, Mathew   138
Allen Court   90
Amberley Museum Railway   124
Ambush point, North Street   147
Amplifon   151-153
Anti-tank ditch   29, 47, 49, 51, 150
ARP   47, 52-55, 62-65, 115
Ashcombe, Lord   41
Ashcombe School   55, 66-69
Ashworth, H   145
Atherton, Kathy   16
atte Pyppe, Alicia   63
atte Pyppe, Walter   63
Aube, Admiral   41
Aubrey, John   10, 25-26
Austen, Jane   20

B
Back-alley   130
Battle of Dorking, The   41
Baker's Garage   55
Baker, W   85
Baptist Chapel   101-102
Barclays Bank   159
Baron's Garage   55
Baron, The   158
Bartholemews Press & Builders   74
Beard, Tony   29
Beehive, The   150
Bechstein's Bat   129
Bellarmine jugs   159
Bell Hotel, The   149-150, 153
Bembridge House   54
Benwicke, I   145
Betchworth Castle   11, 34-37, 160
Betchworth Chalkpits   121-124, 160
Betchworth Station   121
Black Horse, The   139
Blacks II   87
Blanchard, Messrs   125
Bloomfield   19
Blyton, Enid   49
Board of Guardians of the Poor   152
Bolland's   74

Boorers   148
Boots Chemist   19
Boots Opticians   57-60
Bothell, Ephraim   13
Bothell, Thomas   13
Borinie   79
Bourne, Colour Sergeant   9
Bourneside Gallery   147
Bovington Tank Museum   50
Boxall Brewery   106
Box Hill fort/mobilisation centre   41-45
Box Hill pillboxes   45, 50-52, 57
Box Hill water tanks   110-111
Brandram, AG   159
Brannan, Peter James   126
Brayley, William   10, 107
Britannia   108
Bright, JS   121, 138
British Brick Society   92
Brockham Lime Works   121, 124-127
Brown, Geo S   145
Brown, J Dundas   116
Brown, Sir Adam   155
Bull's Head, The   144
Burford Bridge   108-109
Burford Lodge   109-110
Burford Meadow   109
Butcher, Albert Henry   126
Butter Hill House   9, 21-22
Byron, Lord   26

C
Caffyn   159
Caird, J   129
Camden, William   108
Cameron, Ian   148-149
Canute, King   96
Cape Passage   151-152
Carstone   13
Casement, Sir Roger   27
Castle Mill   111, 150
Caveman Barbeque   90
Cawley's Mine   124
Cellar Club, The   97
Chalkpit Lane   121
Chalkpit Terrace   121
Chart, John   152
Chart Park   26-27, 36
Cheesman   19
Chelsea Speleological Society   11, 32, 81, 88, 108, 118, 124, 128, 135
Chesney, George Tompkins   41-42
Chequers Inn, The   92, 143
Chevertons   118
Chitty's butchers   55
Churchill, Winston   28
Church Passage   57-58

Churches of Dorking Housing
    Association 81
Clack, C   85
Clark, Arthur 126
Cliftonville 127, 129-131
Cockfighting 124-135, 157
Cockpit 134-136
Coldharbour Lane 115
Coleman, Miss 108
Constable Court 115
Cotmandene 53, 63, 158
Cotmandene Cottage 158
Courthouse, The 115
Cotton, Elizabeth, Lady Hope 72-73
Covenanter tank 49-50
Cox, William 126
Cricketers, The 72, 81-82
Cure, The 113
Curtis, Dr 116
Crowney, Myles 127
Crypt, The 97

D
Daniel, Casimiy 78-79
Davis, Elaine 88
Deadly Assassin, The 158
Deepdene bunker (Southern Railways)
    26, 28-34
Deepdene East Cave 26, 28-29, 32
Deepdene House 25-32
Deepdene Park air raid shelter 57,
    62-63
Defoe, Daniel 25, 109, 154-155
Denbies 41, 49-50, 158
De Vere Wotton Park Hotel 37
Devonshire, Duke of 79
Dickens, Charles 7, 86, 144
Dietsch kilns 122
Dinnage, William 59, 73, 89, 106, 152
Disraeli, Benjamin 28
Dixon's 86
Doctor Who 158
Dorking Advertiser 17, 53-54, 57, 59,
    65-66, 93, 159
Dorking, a History of the Town 138
Dorking Alterations 143-146
Dorking and Leith Hill Preservation
    Society 22
Dorking: A Surrey Market Town
    through Twenty Centuries 139
Dorking Gas Company 98
Dorking House Antiques 73-74
Dorking Book Shop 141
Dorking Caves. See 'South Street
    Caves'
Dorking Chalkpits 121, 127, 157
Dorking Foundry 92
Dorking Greystone Lime Company
    124
Dorking Halls 62, 66
Dorking in the Great War 16
Dorking Lime 121
Dorking Market 86, 105, 115, 133,
    139-140
Dorking Museum 23, 66, 79, 91-93,
    160

Dorking Omnibus 73
Dorking Stoves 72
Dorking Tool Hire 75
Dorking Travel 89-90
Dorking Urban Council Ratepayers'
    Association 53
Dorking Urban District Council 18,
    54
Dorking Water Company 108
Dorking Waterworks 107-108
Downey V, R, I Overlong, "M" 78
Downs and The Sea, The 124
Downs Solicitors 115, 118
Doubleday's 86
Dragons' teeth 29, 34-35, 47
Drill Hall 41
Duke of Norfolk 25
Dunkirk 44, 50
Dunn's furriers 55
Dunster 138
Dutch House 86

E
Eden, Dorking. See 'Deepdene House'
Ede, Robert Best 106-107
Edit, The 147-148
Emma 20
Emmerson, Andrew 29
Ettlinger, Vivienne 18
Evans, Miss 53
Evelyn, John 10, 25, 37
Evening Star, The 106, 140

F
Falkland Road 93
Farnborough Cottages 89
Farnborough Passage 58, 87-88,
    90-91
Father Ted 158
Fielder's, R 71
Fifth Monarchy Men 11
Fisher, William 126
Fitzroy, Emily 158
Fleming, Dr Michael 74
Flowers by Elaine 87
Folkestone Sand 7, 130
Forman, William Henry 63
Foxbury Shaw 109
Foxenden Quarry air raid shelter 54
Frankenstein 26, 85
Friends of Deepdene 33

G
Garth, The 55
Gentleman's Magazine 80, 99
George Inn 151-152
George V, King 123
Gilbert Scott, Sir George 63
Grayson, Victor 27
Great House on Butter Hill, The 18
Green, Elizabeth 148
Gregory, J Maundy 27-28, 158
Gregory, Pope 96
Grice's bakery 55
Gun Inn 147
Gyle, Eliza 126

H
Hall, John 18
Hamilton, Lady 7
Hand-Book of Dorking, A 9, 18, 96,
    121, 144
Harmans Bespoke Furniture 73
Harper, Charles 124
Hart Scales & Hodges 117
Harvey, Arnold 126
Hearthstone 121, 124-126
Henley Cables 158
Heritage Open Days 22, 60, 73, 116,
    160
Hewett, Ann 85
Higgins, Beryl 18
Higgins, Martin 34, 37
Highways and Byways in Surrey 144
History of The Church and Parish of
    St Martin's Dorking, A 96
Hoffmann kilns 122
Hogg, Miles 84
Hole in the Wall 80-81
Hollier's Teas 73
Hollier, William 73
Home Guard Fieldcraft Manual, The
    49
Home Guard Training School 49
Hope, Henry 36
Hope, Thomas 26-27
Howard, Leslie 140
House by the Well 71
Howard, Charles 18, 25, 30, 33
Hunt Group 113

I
Icehouse 27, 39
Irish Republican Brotherhood 27
ITC 158
ITC white jag 158

J
Jay's 55
Johnson, Ron 61
Jones 85
Journal of the Plague Year, A 155

K
Kendall and Sons 159
Kershaw, JC 124
King, Mrs Elsie 123
Kingham, HG 19
King's Arms, The   153-155
King's Head, The 7, 143-147
Knights Templar 84
Knight, William 126
Kuoni 33
Kuoni Shop 89

L
Labelliere/Labilliere, Major Peter
    79-80
Laker, Henry 126
Langdon-Davies, John 49
Lasletts 118
Lemon Tree, The 151-152
Limeway 121

Lister, Patti 20
Little Dudley House 119
Lloyd of the C.I.D. 158
London and County Bank 151
London Boot Company 151
London Labour and the London Poor 134
London Road 150
London's Secret Tubes 29
Lost Pubs Project 135
Lower Chequers, The 143
Lower Greensand 7
Lloyd George, David 27
Loyns Luncheon Rooms 72
Lucock 89
Lynn, J 145
Lyons Court road 93

M
Mackrell, Robert 126
Magistrates' Court 115
Maison Marcelle 55
Malthouse Antiques 60
Malthouse, The 106
Mason's 92
Marquis of Granby, The 7, 144
Mathews, HS 136
Mausolea and Monuments Trust 33
Maybank, John 135
Mayflower, The 100
Mayhew, Henry 134
Meadowbank Park 12, 105
Metherell, JK 118
Methodist Church 55, 97
Mickleham 108
Mill Lane 105-106
Milton Court 158
Milton Motors 55-57
Mitchell, Andrew 141
Mobilisation centres 42, 44
Montague Burton 57-59
Mole Valley District Council 22, 33, 64
Molyneux, John 48, 66
Moores Road 93, 115
Mount House 75-80
Mullins, William 100

N
Narnia Room 140
National Trust 19, 45, 128, 160
New Fountain Garden Restaurant 74
Nelson, Admiral 7
Newland, William 20
Nissen huts 47-48, 160
Norbury Park House 19
Norden, John 108
Holmwood 11
Nower, the 47-49, 53, 160

O
Old Courthouse, the 115
Old House at Home, The 140, 142
Old Pump House, The 108
Orange Café 118
Order of St John of Jerusalem 84

P
Page, Tony 110
Palmerston's follies 41
Paper Mews 56, 101
Parker, Eric 43, 144
Patching, Resta 108
Patching, Thomas 99, 108
Pebblecombe Hill 124
Pétain, Philippe 50
Peters, Joseph 127
Pevsner, Nikolaus 32
Pickwick Papers, The 7, 144
Picturesque Promenade Round Dorking, A 9, 121, 158
Picturesque Surrey 35, 42
Pilgrim Cottage 80
Pillboxes 45, 47, 50-52, 55, 150, 158, 160
Pimlott, John 135
Pipp Brook, The 7, 105-108
Pippbrook (House) 53-54, 62-66, 92
Pippbrook Mill 111-113
Pixham Mill 111
Pizza Piazza 119
Plan International 49
Policeman's Hole, Mickleham 108-109
Polidori, John 26
Pollock, Hugh 49
Powell Corderoy School, Norfolk Road 66
Powell, James 126
Pump Corner 71-72, 91

Q
Quaker Meeting House 99-101
Queen's Arms 147
Quick's 55

R
Railway Gazette 29
Ram Alley 141
Ram Inn, The 139, 141
Recollections of Old Dorking 17, 106
Red Lion Inn/Hotel, The 87, 93, 140, 159
Reigate Caves 54, 129, 160
Reigate Castle 16
Riddle of the Sands, The 41
Riot, 1830 37, 140, 157
River Mole 7, 41, 47, 51, 80, 108-110, 150, 160
Riverside Care and Support 81
Robert Dyas 92
Rock beerhouse and brewery 89, 91, 140
Rogers, Mark 69
Rorke's Drift 9
Rose and Crown 137
Rose, Charles 17, 36, 106, 115, 139
Rose Hill House 20, 74, 116
Rosse, Edith 27

S
Sainsbury's 87, 91-93
St Catherine's Hospice Shop 147-149

St Martin's Church 16, 59, 79, 95-99, 105, 107
St Martin's intermediate church 96, 107
St Martin's Walk 55
St Saviours Dispersed scheme 81
Salomons, Leopold 19
Salter and Baxter, Messrs 131
Sauberge's 92
Scotts of Dorking 60, 87-89
Scream and Scream Again 157
Secret Intelligence Service 27
Selman, Mr 136-137
Shoerite 143-144
Six-pounder gun 51-52
Skipton Building Society 91
Smidth kiln 122
Smith, Victor 42
Soane, Sir John 35
Society of Friends 99
Southern Railways Traffic Control Centre. See Deepdene bunker
South Street Caves 8-19, 22-23, 32, 76-77, 84-87, 92, 128, 130, 134, 160
Sowan, Paul 126, 127, 130
Spanish Civil War 49
Spratley, Elizabeth 106
Spring Gardens 105-106
Star, The 140, 142
Star and Garter Hotel, The (now The Lincoln Arms) 53
Stedman, John Ellis 18
Stepping Stones 51
Stone & Turner 21, 92
Subterranea Britannica 69
Sun Inn, The 83, 138-140
Surrey Antique Bottle Collectors' Club 159
Surrey Bat Group 45, 128
Surrey County Council 54, 64, 68
Surrey County Council air raid shelters 54, 68
Surrey Mirror 18, 93, 130, 136, 138, 159
Surrey Yeoman, The 142-143
Surrey Wildlife Trust 33, 128
Swallets/Swallows/Swallowholes 108-110, 160
Swayne, John 78-79

T
Talbot House 138-139, 153
Tank trap 29, 147
Tank trap, river 51
Taylerson, Major 124
Temperance Hotel 72-73
Terrornauts, The 158
Tett Turret 158
TG Rix's 72
Things To Come 62
Thompson, Gibson 35, 42
Three Tuns, The 139
Timbs, John 9, 18, 25
Time Gentlemen Please: the Story of Dorking Pubs 141, 151
Times, The 26
Tombs, Sue 79

Topographical History of Surrey, A   10,
    106-107, 109
*Tour thro' the Whole Island of Great
    Britain, A*   154
Town Destructor   108
Tucker, Abraham   35
Tudor Williams   87
Turner, B, Messrs   53, 55

U
United Reform Church   101-103
Upstairs, Downstairs   20, 117

V
Vampyre, The   26
Victoria Terrace   18-19
Victoria, Queen   106
Villa Deodati   26
Viva restaurant   137

W
Waitrose   55, 74, 141, 158
Walker, Mary   13
War of the Worlds, The   41
Washway, The   105
Water sousey   86, 144
Wealden Cave and Mine Society   129
Weller, Sam   144
Well, Pump Corner   105
Well, Roman, St Martin's Church   96,
    99
Wells, South Street Caves   9, 14-16
Well, White Horse   84-86
Wells, HG   62
Westcott air raid shelter, Chapel Lane
    60-61, 160
Westhumble air raid shelter, Pilgrim's
    Way   57, 61-62
Westhumble Mine   127-130
Wheatsheaf, The   19, 83, 133-138, 142
When William Came   41
White Hart, The   141-143, 160
White Horse Hotel   83-86, 149
White Lion, The   147-149
White's   87
WH Smith   139
Wickes   66
Wilkinson, Mr   54
Williams, J   145
Williams, Vaughan   66
Wine and Spirit Trade Record   17
Wintringham, Tom   49
Witchcraft   13
Women's Voluntary Service   62
Woodcock's   86
Wood, Elizabeth   13
Wotton House   27, 37-39

Y
Ye Old Oake Shop   148
Young, Heathfield   79
Young, Henry Harman   16
Young's   19

Z
Zhivotovsky, David Leonteivich   27